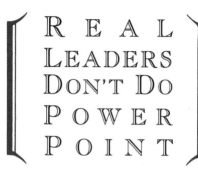

REAL
LEADERS
DON'T DO
POWER
POINT

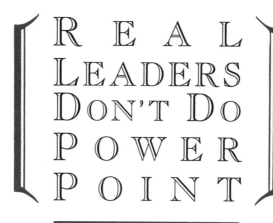

REAL LEADERS DON'T DO POWER POINT

HOW TO SELL YOURSELF AND YOUR IDEAS

Christopher Witt

with Dale Fetherling

CROWN
BUSINESS
NEW YORK

Published in the United States by Crown Business,
an imprint of the Crown Publishing Group,
a division of Random House, Inc., New York.
www.crownpublishing.com

CROWN BUSINESS is a trademark and
CROWN and the Rising Sun colophon are
registered trademarks of Random House, Inc.

Library of Congress Cataloging-in-Publication Data

Witt, Christopher, 1951–
    Real leaders don't do PowerPoint / Christopher Witt.—1st ed.
        p.   cm.
    1. Public speaking.   2. Leadership.   I. Title.
    PN4129.15.W58 2009
    808.5'1—dc22   2008034138

ISBN 978-0-307-40770-2

Printed in the United States of America
Book Design by Robert C. Olsson
10 9 8 7 6 5 4 3 2 1
First Edition

To Ray Valli

CONTENTS

PART FOUR: A MASTERFUL DELIVERY

CONTENTS

EXEMPLARY SPEECHES

WHY LEADERS AREN'T
LIKE OTHER PEOPLE

L eaders aren't like other people—at least not when it comes to giving speeches. Other people try to get out of giving a speech any way they can. They put off preparing for it until the last minute, then fire up PowerPoint, and create slides that are just like the slides they've seen every other presenter use. They happily stand in the dark, cede center stage to a screen on which they project those slides, and more often than not, read them word for word to audiences who furtively check their phones and PDAs. Other people are relieved simply to get through a presentation without embarrassing themselves.

But if you're a leader, you must look and sound like a leader in every speech you give. There's too much riding on your performance—your prestige, your ability to command people's attention and support, the success of your project or your organization—to settle for being average.

If you're working your way up, one of the best ways to position yourself as a leader in the eyes of others is to speak like a leader. Just because everyone else shies away from giving speeches or relies too much on PowerPoint is no reason for you to. As a matter of fact, it's a good reason *not* to. You need to set yourself apart from other people.

Even if you aren't a leader and you harbor no strong desire to be one, you may be tired of having your ideas dismissed while other people's ideas, less compelling than yours, win a better hearing and get a more positive response. If so, you can learn from the way leaders speak and use their techniques and strategies to improve the impact of what you say.

Remember, audiences don't want leaders to speak like everyone else. They hold leaders to a higher standard, demanding more of them. And leaders expect more of themselves too, knowing that just being a good speaker isn't good enough. They want their speeches to advance their organization's success and to promote their personal status.

So whether you are a leader, an aspiring leader, or simply someone who wants to be taken more seriously, you need to speak better and more intelligently than other people. You can't jot down some talking points at the last moment—or rely on someone else to do it for you—and say whatever comes to mind. You can't trust PowerPoint to make your point. You can't just troll for stories and quotes from the Internet to sprinkle through your speech. Instead, you need to let yourself shine through. You've got to make your thoughts, your convictions, your vision, and your character manifest themselves in what you say.

Why, exactly, do leaders need to be different?

- **Leaders speak when a lot is at stake.**

In times of crisis, change, or opportunity—when expectations are high and the consequences may be momentous—that's when people turn to leaders for words of insight, reassurance, or direction. After a national tragedy, for instance, the country waits for the president to speak. (Reagan's speech on the evening of the space shuttle *Challenger* disaster—"We will never forget them, nor the last time we saw them, as they prepared for their journey and waved goodbye and 'slipped the surly bonds of earth' to 'touch the face of God'"—helped comfort a stunned nation.) When a company releases a new product, who better to herald it than the leader? And following an acquisition, anxious employees don't know where they stand until they hear the CEO's plans . . . from the CEO's mouth.

Leaders speak to make a difference, and unsettled times are when their words can have the greatest impact.

- **Leaders speak as representatives of their organizations.**

Here's the paradox: Leaders have to be themselves at all times and yet, when they speak, they speak not for themselves, but for their organizations. Inexperienced or ineffective leaders sometimes forget this. They make offhand remarks in public settings or spontaneous asides from the podium, and then they're surprised when people take their comments as policy. But real leaders know that audiences take their words seriously, much more seriously than they take the words of other people. And leaders *want* their words to be taken seriously.

The success of any organization—whether it's a multinational corporation, a nonprofit, a fledgling start-up, a department, a one-person operation—depends on its leader's persuasiveness. Similarly, any project—a launch, a PR campaign, an oral proposal for a large contract—is aided or hobbled by its leader's ability to make its case.

- **Leaders speak all the time.**

Leaders give formal or informal presentations several times a week, if not more often. They speak to the board of directors, to executives, to company-wide gatherings, to the general public, to associations and service clubs, to funding sources, to major clients and potential customers. They appear on panels, on radio and television, and in print. A recent survey of 100 Fortune 1,000 companies found that their chief executives received an average of 175 invitations a year just to speak at conferences.

Aspiring leaders seek out opportunities to give speeches. They speak up at meetings. They give project updates. They participate in team presentations to prospective clients. They address service clubs and professional associations. They lead teleclasses and webinars.

- **Leaders speak because it's their job.**

Speaking is one of the most important responsibilities of a leader, and real leaders take it on as a challenge and an opportunity.

I most frequently get asked to work with leaders for two reasons. Usually, it's when leaders have a major speech coming up with a lot riding on it, and they have to ace it. But more and more often, I get asked to coach rising stars—people who are being groomed for a promotion, say—because the powers-that-be are dissatisfied with their speaking skills. "We'd like to move our senior scientist into more of a leadership position," they'll say, "but he speaks, no matter what the occasion, like he's giving a technical briefing." Or they'll say, "She's the next CEO we're looking for, but she just doesn't come across to large groups with any kind of charisma."

I also get called in to work with senior researchers, scientists, and engineers, when the people they report to are frustrated by their poor presentation skills. "My people are some of the brightest in the industry," the director of R&D at a high-tech company once told me, "but all their knowledge isn't worth a cent to the company if they can't share it with others." So I tell these "subject matter experts" that in spite of what they may think, knowledge isn't power; communicating knowledge *is*. I tell them that the facts don't speak for themselves; people gather the facts, evaluate them, make sense of them, and speak on their behalf. And I tell them that giving presentations may not be in their job descriptions, but it should be. Their value to the organization isn't in what they know; it's in their ability to present what they know to people in a variety of fields in a way that can be understood and acted upon.

Speaking is one of the best ways for people to position themselves as leaders and to communicate what they know in a way that gets a favorable response.

- **Leaders speak to influence and inspire.**

I always ask my clients to describe the most powerful speech they can remember hearing from a leader. What did the leader do, I ask, that made that speech so impressive? Their answers vary, although they inevitably touch upon similar elements: the leader's sense of presence, conviction, passion, quick wit or ready humor, ability to reach out and touch the audience, masterful delivery, and—most of all—an engaging and memorble message. In all the times I've asked the question, never once has anyone answered, "I liked how the speaker used PowerPoint."

And there's a reason for that.

Professionals and academicians often debate the merits of Power-Point. Both sides of the argument have one thing in common: They assume its purpose is to transmit information. And that's precisely why leaders—real leaders—want little to do with it. Because they aren't primarily concerned with communicating information. They speak to promote a vision, a direction, or a passion. They're seeking to influence and inspire. And no one thinks PowerPoint is the way to do that.

True, if you're making a report, conducting a training session, or leading a seminar, communicating information becomes more critical. But it should never be the sole or even the primary reason you're speaking. Speak like a leader and you'll present information not for its own sake, but in a way that shapes how the audience thinks about it and influences how they act on it.

THE FOUR ELEMENTS

Almost 2,500 years ago Demosthenes, the father of Greek oratory, cited four elements of a great speech: (1) a great person, (2) a noteworthy event, (3) a compelling message, and (4) a masterful delivery. Those four elements are as pertinent today as they were in ancient Greece. And this book is divided into those four main parts.

To be *a great person* you don't have to be the president of the United States or even the president of your company. You might be a department head interested in building a cohesive team, focused on a shared goal. Or a self-employed consultant, coach, architect, or financial planner building your practice by speaking to select audiences. Or a sales rep tired of sounding like—and being treated like—every other sales rep. Or a community leader with a cause or a candidate you want to promote. Or a technical expert working your way out of the laboratory. It doesn't matter. You have to be the best *you* you can be. So let your experience, passion, character, and even your sense of humor show up in every word you say and how you say it.

Similarly, you should only be involved with *noteworthy events*. Sometimes that means turning down speaking opportunities that aren't worth your time or that would cheapen people's perception of your authority. And sometimes that means working with the people responsible for the event to refine its purpose, schedule, and setting.

A *compelling message* is nothing more—and nothing less—than an idea with the power to change people's lives, if only in a small way, expressed in the clearest, most compelling words. It takes diligent preparation. There's no shortcut. Leaders who stand in front of an audience and wing it don't get respect and don't deserve it.

Doc Pomus—the legendary songwriter who created "A Teenager in Love," "Suspicion," and "Save the Last Dance for Me"—was once asked how to write a hit song. He answered, "Find the shortest distance between your insides and a pencil." He could have said the same thing about creating a compelling message. Leaders find the shortest distance between their insides and an audience's ears.

A *masterful delivery* depends on any number of elements, such as planting your feet, making eye contact, and projecting your voice. But it's so much more than technique. It's really about projecting yourself—your authentic self—in the most powerful way possible.

Other people may settle for, say, two out of the four elements and think they're doing pretty well. But not you. You're a leader or aspire to be one. And you know that being a good-enough speaker doesn't cut it. You want to be exceptional. That drive is what has gotten you where you are today . . . and will take you where you want to go.

And if you take this book's advice to heart, you are likely to get there faster by being a more confident, more commanding, more compelling speaker.

PART ONE

[A GREAT
PERSON]

You Are the Message

Who you are is inseparable from what you communicate. I don't just mean that your actions speak louder than your words. Of course they do. I mean that your character—who you are, what you've done, what you value—shapes the message your listeners hear.

Take Donald Trump. What do we know about him? That he's a domineering alpha male with a bad haircut and an outsized ego who's in headlong pursuit of riches and fame no matter what the consequences. If he gave a talk about altruism or touchy-feely customer service, would you believe him?

On the other hand, consider Herb Kelleher, the cofounder and former CEO of Southwest Airlines. Eccentric and fun-loving, he was known for sometimes loading luggage or taking tickets at the gate, for putting employees first, customers second, and his board of directors third. Can you imagine him giving Trump's speech . . . or Trump giving his?

If Trump told a gathering of his employees that he loves them, they'd throw up. Kelleher, on the other hand, used what he called the "L word" all the time, and his employees once took out a full-page ad to tell him how much they adored him. Both have been successful in business. But neither could give the other's speech with any integrity.

Mary Kay Ash, the founder of Mary Kay Cosmetics, could have spoken about women helping women succeed in business, but not about being a stay-at-home mom. Bill Gates could talk about the future of the Internet or even philanthropy, but could never give a speech titled "Small Is Beautiful."

That's because speakers are only credible when what they say is in sync with who they are.

When your message is at odds with who you are—or, at least, with who the audience perceives you to be—two problems arise. First, you'll have trouble delivering your message. You'll feel, at best, like an actor playing a part or, at worst, like a fraud. You'll lose your spontaneity, confidence, and authenticity. And second, your audience won't believe it. They'll doubt what you say and, even more damning, they'll doubt *you*.

A client of mine—let's call her Jenny—is president of a consulting firm she built from a one-person shop to a million-dollar business. She marketed her services by speaking to targeted audiences, establishing herself as an authority in the eyes of prospective clients. She described herself as dynamic, driven, and straitlaced. A colleague called her "Martha Stewart with a sense of humor."

She had previously worked with physicians who wanted to build their practices. Now she wanted to attract more clients by working with chiropractors as well. Her research gave her confidence that the same strategies that helped physicians would help chiropractors. It also taught her she'd have to tweak her message, making it more suited to her new audience.

But after giving a number of talks to chiropractors, she was disappointed with the response. "If I were talking to physicians," she said, "I'd be getting a lot more prospective clients wanting appointments to talk with me." She hired me to sit in on her next presentation and give her feedback.

I'd already seen her speak to physicians, so I could understand why they responded so well to her. She took the stage with confidence, projected an upbeat attitude, and spoke engagingly without notes. She poked fun at doctors in a way that got them laughing at themselves. And they *loved* her.

When she talked one-on-one with the chiropractors before her speech, I could see they were equally impressed by her. But once she began her talk, she seemed less sure of herself. She anchored herself behind the lectern and kept referring to her notes. And she was entirely humorless. The audience applauded politely when she finished, but almost no one went up to talk to her.

Afterward, I asked her why she had taken that approach. "Chiropractors tend to be looser, more right-brained, less uptight types of people than physicians," she said. "So I want to project a warmer, less in-your-face image."

It wasn't working, I told her. And I advised her to speak the same way she always did. "You can adapt your message—within limits—to suit a different audience," I said. "But you can't change *you*."

The next time she spoke she strode out to center stage, looked her listeners straight in the eye, and laid out her program with an unassuming air of authority. Admitting she was more accustomed to talking to physicians, she made a quip about the difference between the two professions, ribbing chiropractors for their image. They laughed. And afterward many of them clustered around to speak with her.

Leaders adapt what they say—changing emphasis here and there, substituting examples or stories when appropriate—to better address the needs and concerns of different audiences. But they shouldn't change themselves or try to become someone else.

Thus, it's critical to know yourself and, more important, to know how you are perceived. Be yourself, because you can't be anyone else anyway. And let your true self come through in what you talk about and in how you talk about it.

General George S. Patton, for example, honed a theatrical image. He wore a highly polished helmet, riding breeches, and knee-high cavalry boots. He sported ivory-handled, nickel-plated revolvers. His aggressive warrior image totally aligned with his actions on the battlefield.

He riddled his tough-talking speeches with irreverence and profanity as a way to bond with and inspire his troops. You may remember the speech delivered by actor George C. Scott at the beginning of the film *Patton*. A sanitized version of the real thing, it began, "Now, I want you to remember that no bastard ever won a war by dying for his country. He won it by making the other poor dumb bastard die for his country." He continued:

Now, there's one thing that you men will be able to say when you get back home, and you may thank God for it. Thirty years from now when you're sitting around your fireside with your grandson on your knee, and he asks you, "What did you do in the great

World War Two?" You won't have to say, "Well, I shoveled shit in Louisiana." All right now, you sons of bitches, you know how I feel. I will be proud to lead you wonderful guys into battle anytime, anywhere. That's all.

The harsh way Patton spoke mirrored the way he was known for leading his troops. He successfully matched his image to his message, and his message to his audience. In fact, upon his death, more than 20,000 soldiers reportedly volunteered to be his pallbearers.

Contrast that with another famous general, George Washington. In 1783, officers of the bedraggled revolutionary army were hatching a plot. They'd heard that the fledgling government was broke and unable to pay them.

Washington knew, no matter how legitimate their grievances, that their insurrection would mean the end of the republic. He walked uninvited into their angry gathering and for nearly half an hour argued for their loyalty with little success.

At the end of his speech, he opened a letter from a member of Congress, which detailed the earnest efforts being made to pay the young nation's debts. Washington squinted, held the letter at arm's length, and then fell silent. The officers looked at one another, puzzled.

Finally, the general reached into his coat and took out a pair of glasses. The officers had never seen their physically formidable commander with glasses. "Gentlemen," he apologized, "you will permit me to put on my spectacles, for I have not only grown gray but almost blind in the service of my country."

His humbling admission achieved what his rhetoric had not. Some of the officers wept, and in the words of his biographer, "from behind the shining drops, their heads looked with love at the commander who had led them all so far and long." Talk of rebellion ended on the spot, because Washington had dared to reveal his true self, a self very different from Patton's but equally powerful in its much less dramatic way.

MATCHING YOUR MESSAGE TO YOUR REPUTATION

First, you have to know what your reputation is. That's harder to discern than you'd think. The problem is, the higher you rise in an organization, the less willing people are to tell you what they really think of you. So you're better off asking your peers, leaders like yourself who have little to gain by pulling their punches. Or hire an executive coach, someone whose job it is to be honest. Or if all else fails, ask your kids.

Second, you have to know what image you project when you speak. Every time you speak you tell the audience who you are. And not just by the words you choose but by all the other signals you send out: your facial expressions, your eyes, your posture, your voice, your intensity, your sense of humor, your choice of anecdotes, how you treat your listeners, and many other intangibles. You may think you're projecting yourself in a particular way. But how do you really know? The best—and most humbling—way to find out is to watch a video of yourself. First time through, turn down the volume and look only at your face and your eyes—they communicate almost 80 percent of how you come across. Then watch it again, this time on fast-forward. Doing so will highlight your movements and gestures—the remaining 20 percent of your nonverbal communication.

And the last thing you must do is to stop doing certain things. Stop imitating any other speaker, even someone you greatly admire. Stop sounding like a corporate clone. (Using words or phrases like *best of breed, change agent, impactful, results-driven, going forward, paradigm shift, mission critical*, or *value-added* is a sure way to kill your authenticity.) And stop saying what other people think. Take a contrarian position. Argue against the conventional wisdom of the day. Stake out a new position and defend it with all you've got. When you stop trying to look or sound or think like everyone else and start just being yourself, your reputation and your image will take care of themselves.

Bombarded with signals, your listeners make judgments about what you stand for and what, really, your message is. The words themselves are meaningless unless the rest of you backs them up. So the first rule of public speaking is this: You are a walking, talking message. Everything about you and everything the audience knows about you supports—or refutes—what you say.

So before you take to the platform, make sure that what you want to say and how you say it resonate with who you are. And remember: you're not just the messenger, you're the message.

You Only Have Three Speeches

Other people may speak to communicate information. But *not* you. You're a leader (or aspire to be one), and leaders have loftier goals. Leaders speak for one of three reasons:

- **To identify**—tell audiences who they are or who they can become.
- **To influence**—shape the way audiences think and feel.
- **To inspire**—make audiences want to act.

As a leader it's up to you to communicate a vision, a direction, a purpose, and the impetus for acting. The more you focus on imparting facts and figures, the less you'll be perceived as a leader.

- **To identify**

Leaders tell their listeners (or remind them when they seem to have forgotten) who they are—what binds them together, what makes them unique, what sets them apart from others.

Political leaders are always doing this. They are always defining who "we" are, whether the "we" is partisan ("we Democrats" or "we

Republicans") or inclusive ("we Americans"). That's what Robert F. Kennedy did on the night Martin Luther King Jr. was assassinated. Against the advice of his staff, he waded into an inner-city crowd of mainly African-Americans and gave them the terrible news. He spoke to them about what they had in common, reminding them how he, more than most, knew the pain of losing someone he loved to an assassin's bullet. But he urged his listeners to rise above tragedy: "In this difficult day, in this difficult time for the United States, it's perhaps well to ask what kind of a nation we are and what direction we want to move in."

Military leaders do the same thing. Marine drill sergeants know that they are teaching recruits not just the skills and techniques of warfare, they're also inculcating an identity. They're teaching the values, traditions, and moral character of "the few, the proud, the Marines." General Douglas MacArthur, speaking at West Point, did the same thing, emphasizing shared, core values to those preparing to become Army officers: "Duty, honor, country."

Business leaders do the same thing, too. They talk about the organization's values and history, its unique approach or style, its accomplishments. They're always saying in one form or another, directly or indirectly, "This is who we are or should be or can be."

For example, when Meg Whitman, then-CEO of eBay, spoke to the international convention "eBay Live" in 2005, she briefly traced the company's history and its founder's vision. She noted who was in attendance—people from all fifty states and from sixty-two countries. And she announced the conference's theme: "The Power of All of Us." Her entire speech was about "us" and about who "we" are.

IDENTIFYING THE GROUP

For corporations and companies, identity and mission are almost always indistinguishable. Business speakers can get at the root of identity by asking:

Who are we? What unites us? What sets us apart and makes us unique?

What's our history? How have we evolved?

Who are our founders? What motivated them? What was their vision?

What service or products do we provide? How have they progressed?

Who benefits from what we do? Who are our clients/customers? How have they changed over the years?

How does who we are shape what we do? How does what we do shape who we are?

"eBay is much more than an online marketplace where people buy and sell," Whitman said. "It is a real society, a thriving community of people who are tapping the power of the Internet."

So if you're giving an "identity" speech, stress what you have in common with your listeners and what they have in common with one another, whether it's your values, history, or mission. Tell them what makes them different from others and better than others. Then challenge them to be even better.

- **To influence**

Influence isn't about telling listeners *what* to think and feel about a specific issue. It's about shaping *how* they think and feel about issues in general. Once you do that, it's easier to get them to take the action you'd like them to take.

Leaders have a vision or a dream—a compelling image of a better future. And they speak tirelessly, relentlessly—some would say fanatically—to make their audiences see what they see. That requires igniting the audience's imagination, something that PowerPoint fails to do. It can display words, charts, graphs, illustrations, photographs, and even audio-video segments. But what it can't do is excite the imagination.

Take Martin Luther King's dream of a day when "on the red hills of Georgia the sons of former slaves and the sons of former slave owners will be able to sit down together at a table of brotherhood." Would Power-Point have helped his audience see what he saw? Even if PowerPoint had existed in his day and even if there had been a way to project an image large enough for 500,000 marchers to see, what could King have shown? Nothing, because what he saw did not yet exist. And any image that could have been created would have been a pale and lifeless reflection of what was in his mind's eye.

In business, influence and vision are linked. Steve Jobs, Apple's company evangelist and brand spokesperson, gives electrifying presentations. That's because he doesn't just sell chips and circuitry, operating systems and hardware; he sells an experience. He promotes not technology, but what technology can do for his audience. When he introduced the 30GB iPod, for example, he explained not how it worked but how it would improve listeners' lives by giving them access to 7,500 songs, 25,000 photos, and up to 75 hours of video.

Even though Apple's share of the computer market is small, its influence is vast. And that's due in no small measure to Jobs's vision and his passion for communicating it to others. His audiences see what he sees and like what they see.

Anita Roddick, founder and former CEO of The Body Shop, also electrified audiences. That's because she didn't talk about skin care and moisturizing lotions—the "stuff" of her business. Instead, she talked passionately and tirelessly about the opportunities businesses have not just to do well, but to do good. Roddick's vision is summed up in the opening statement of The Body Shop's mission statement: "To dedicate our business to the pursuit of social and environmental change."

Roddick was knighted by Queen Elizabeth in 2003, and the following year The Body Shop was voted the second most trusted brand in the United Kingdom. And that was largely due to Roddick's vision and her passion for communicating what she sees to others.

What is your vision? Can you make it concrete and specific, while at the same time keeping it evocative and attractive? How does it inform the way you look upon the world? See it first in your imagination. Then project it into the hearts and minds of your audience. That's how you'll win influence.

- **To inspire**

To inspire is to kindle your listeners' desire to act. Inspiration, literally, means to "breathe into." In this case, to breathe life and vitality into your audience. You do that not by giving them step-by-step instructions but by giving them a motive, a desire to act. You give them the hope that they can achieve what they want. "If you want to build a ship, don't drum up the men to gather the wood, divide the work, and give orders," wrote Antoine de Saint-Exupéry, aviator and author of *The Little Prince*. "Instead, teach them to yearn for the vast and endless sea."

Military leaders before a battle, political leaders in time of crisis, coaches during halftime, preachers all the time—they know that what people often need is not more instruction, but more inspiration, not more "how to," but more "you *can*." And successful leaders in every other endeavor know it, too.

In 1963 Mary Kay Ash founded Mary Kay Cosmetics in a Dallas storefront with $5,000. Nine "beauty consultants" (saleswomen) sold products door to door. The business grew to over one and a half million salespeople in thirty-two countries, helped by Mary Kay's relentless optimism, generous incentives (the famous pink Cadillacs), and inspirational, almost evangelical, talks. She believed in women's ability to succeed and in helping them believe in themselves. "You can have anything in this world you want," she used to tell them, "if you want it badly enough and you're willing to pay the price."

When she died, the president of sales and marketing for her company paid tribute to her: "She never cared, quite frankly about how big her business was—she cared about the women and that's her legacy. She said it wasn't about profit and loss, it's about people and love. She gave women in her company a sense of confidence and belief in themselves."

Know your audience. Know their concerns, fears, frustrations, and—more important—their hopes and dreams. Don't tell them what they should do or what they should feel. Instead, give them reason to believe in taking action. Give them hope that by acting they can better their lives and the world around them. Then stand back and be amazed at what they do.

As a leader you give any number of speeches, not just formal ones to packed auditoriums. You also welcome guests, make toasts, introduce other speakers or dignitaries, pay tribute to someone or speak at a retirement ceremony, give impromptu pep talks, and on and on. But here's the trick: Those speeches, no matter how different they are, are a variation of the three speeches leaders ever really give. Those speeches allow you to remind your audiences who they are or can be, to show them a new way of seeing the world, or even a world they haven't yet imagined, and to stir them up by speaking not just to their heads but to their hearts and their imaginations.

TAKE A STAND

If you're going to go to all the trouble of preparing and giving a talk, you might as well say what you strongly believe, something an audience needs and wants to hear.

In fact, as a leader or aspiring leader, you're expected to have a strong point of view. You're being counted on to unfurl a bold banner, not just meekly wave the same little flag everyone else does.

To raise your banner, you'll need to rise above the day-to-day clatter and set out strong, overarching principles. After all, did Lincoln recount the battle when he stepped upon the stage at Gettysburg? No. Did Mother Teresa enumerate the pros and cons of selfless love? No. Did JFK detail the myriad programs by which one could serve one's country? No. But they all captured the hearts of their listeners by voicing truths deeply felt, plainly stated, and powerfully delivered.

"When a brave person takes a stand," the Reverend Billy Graham said, "the spines of others are often stiffened."

The stand leaders take is something akin to their character or reputation. It doesn't change from speech to speech. It informs every talk they give. It's their underlying theme, approach, orientation.

There's a lot of talk these days about personal branding. I hate the concept. Neither you nor I are commodities to be packaged and sold. I'd rather speak of taking a stand than of being a brand. But, in truth, they're both about consistently presenting a reliable image to the world.

The difference? Taking a stand is more about principles and the willingness to hold on to them, no matter what. Branding is more a marketing or PR contrivance.

"Here I stand. I can do no other," Martin Luther told King Charles V in refusing to recant his then-iconoclastic religious views. Luther didn't have a brand, but he had his principles and he stuck to them.

Once a prominent politician I was coaching asked my advice on how to answer an important and particularly troublesome question he was expecting from the media. "Tell me where you stand," I replied, "and I'll help you fashion a position statement."

Without pausing, he turned to his chief of staff, and asked "Where *do* I stand on this?" That was our final meeting.

For leaders with more moxie, three basic types of stands exist:

- **Stand *with*.** You stand with people, helping them to know themselves as well as influencing and inspiring them. In the days before the attack by the dreaded Spanish Armada, Queen Elizabeth I was warned against going among her troops, because her advisers feared for her life. But she went anyway, retorting, "I do not desire to live to distrust my faithful and loving people. Let tyrants fear. . . . I am come amongst you at this time, not as for my recreation or sport, but being resolved, in the midst and heat of the battle, to live or die amongst you all."

Similarly, John F. Kennedy in giving his famous *"Ich bin ein Berliner"* speech declared his solidarity with the citizens of the divided city. And Anwar el-Sadat took a courageous stand when he told the Israeli Knesset, "I come to you today on solid ground to shape a new life and to establish peace. All love this land, the land of God; we all, Moslems, Christians, and Jews, all worship God."

To identify with your audience say "I" and "you" and "us." And most of all say "we" and mean it. By identifying with your audience, you establish their identity, which is one of the most important reasons that a leader speaks. You're not just saying, "I am with you." You're saying, "This is who we are—you and I together."

With whom do you align yourself?

• **Stand *for*.** Leaders must stake out clear positions on issues, sometimes even to their detriment. It's easy to stand for security, for happiness, for prosperity, for justice. But what about taking that to the next level and standing for some controversial way of achieving security, happiness, prosperity, or justice?

President Lyndon Johnson, a son of the segregated South, addressed Congress in 1965 and urged it to strike down laws that kept blacks from voting. "I speak tonight for the dignity of man and the destiny of democracy," he said. "There is no constitutional issue here. The command of the Constitution is plain. There is no moral issue. It is wrong—deadly wrong—to deny any of our fellow Americans the right to vote in this country.

There is no issue of states' rights or national rights. There is only the struggle for human rights." Stands don't get much clearer than that.

The deputy director of a state agency periodically made reports to other state agencies, in order to win their approval and to gain their financial backing for huge infrastructure projects. He was rarely successful. His boss asked me to work with him to improve his win rate. Before his next presentation, I listened to what he planned on saying. He clearly outlined the project and its scope. He explained the reasons it was behind schedule. And he discussed three ways to get it back on track. At the end I asked, "So which of the three alternatives are you recommending?" He said it wasn't his responsibility to take a position. "After all," he said, "they have the authority to make the final decision. Not me." "You are the expert," I said. "It's your responsibility to persuade them. Right now you're just giving them options and distancing yourself from the outcome. You have to take a stand and make your best case for it."

You can speak in favor of all sorts of worthy issues, causes, policies, or programs, but your audience will only give you credence when they see that you have a personal stake in the outcome. To advocate change, which is what you're doing when you're speaking for something, without sharing in the risks and the challenges it entails is to sound like a politician making campaign promises.

What position or policy do you advocate?

• **Stand *against.*** Leaders take a strong stand against that which they cannot tolerate. Leaders refuse to gloss over differences or to turn a blind eye to things they consider abhorrent, even in the face of enormous pressure to do so.

Abolitionist and former slave Frederick Douglass was asked to join in a commemoration in 1852 of the signing of the Declaration of Independence. "This Fourth of July is *yours,* not *mine,*" he told his (white) audience. "*You* may rejoice, I must mourn." He went on to give what historians say is probably his most moving speech: "Standing with God and the crushed and bleeding slave on this occasion, I will, in the name of humanity which is outraged, in the name of liberty which is fettered, in the name of the Constitution and the Bible which are disregarded and trampled upon, dare to call in question and to denounce, with all the emphasis I can command, everything that serves to perpetuate slavery."

Taking a stand against something—a policy, an accepted attitude, a way of doing business—is possibly the riskiest thing a leader can do these days. And yet it is one of the most powerful ways both to shape an audience's identity ("this is what *we* can't abide") and to influence its way of thinking ("this is how *not* to think or feel or act").

What person or group, position, policy, rule, or regulation do you oppose?

If you want to be a popular speaker—if the audience's applause is what you value most—avoid saying anything sharp, definitive, or controversial.

Be vague and noncommittal. Figure out what your listeners want you to say and say it. But if you want to speak like a leader, well, that's another thing altogether.

To establish yourself as a leader, you have to be willing to take a stand on even the most controversial issues, a stand that is unequivocal and unwavering. Or, as an old country-song title has it, "You Gotta Stand for Somethin' or You'll Fall for Anything."

CAN CHARISMA BE CAUGHT?

You're sitting at the head table, next in line to speak, and, of course, subtly sizing up your competition. Trouble is, the first person who gets up to talk couldn't be more stunning if she were bathed in sunlight breaking through a dark cloud. She's *terrific*! Poised and in command, she has a strong, rich voice and a relaxed manner, and she offers well-chosen words of awesome impact.

But your envy soon gives way to admiration as you sense her affecting you not just rationally but emotionally. You feel yourself and the audience soaring along with the ideas she presents so passionately. This woman has *it*!

But what is "it"? And can you get some, too?

Charisma is easy to spot but hard to define. I think of it as an innate set of personal attributes that give a person a distinctive "charge," a magnetism, a form of interpersonal power that energizes audiences and influences them viscerally.

The word *charisma*, Greek in origin, means "gift" or "divine favor." And that implies it's not something you can acquire by force of will, by going to a workshop, or by reading *Charisma for Dummies*. (Despite all the help and resources at their disposal, Presidents Ford, Carter, Bush I, and Bush II never became one degree more charismatic.)

People, I think, either are or aren't charismatic. Charisma can't really be learned. But leaders *can* develop more of a commanding presence. Part of that involves tapping into who you really are and connecting—really connecting—to your listeners.

For instance, I once met with an executive who was being groomed to replace the outgoing CEO, a truly charismatic speaker. When the CEO-in-waiting ushered me into his office, the place was abuzz with ringing phones and people scurrying around. He calmly shut his door and told his assistant to hold his calls and postpone any meetings.

Then he shook my hand, looked me in the eye, and for the entire time we were together, gave me his full attention. I felt as if I were the only person who mattered to him at that moment.

Yet when I saw a videotape of him speaking, he looked ill at ease and spoke in a strained, unnecessarily loud voice. When I asked him what his intention in his speech was, he said, "I was trying to channel my CEO."

"What works for him," I replied, "doesn't work for you." This man's gift was connection, not charisma. And that's what I encouraged him to emphasize, because when you connect with yourself, with the audience, and with the moment, you're truly present. And that kind of presence, when you're standing in front of an audience, has a power all its own.

Take Al Gore, for example. As a politician and presidential candidate, he was never what you might call a fiery speaker. Even now, he'd hardly be dubbed charismatic. But many have commented on how his delivery has improved exponentially since he began talking about climate change.

He's more at ease, more personable, and more persuasive. Why? Because he's found something he's passionate about. And his passion comes through loud and clear in his newfound connection with his audiences.

A COMMANDING PRESENCE

Face it: You may not be the sort of speaker who arouses white-hot fervor in your listeners. But here's how you can make yourself more attractive to audiences and project a more commanding presence:

- **Be yourself.** Don't imitate anyone, even dynamic speakers you admire. Everything that makes you unique—from your appearance to your beliefs, your experience, and your sense of humor—can be used in a way that wins people's attention and respect.
- **Be in the moment.** As simple as it sounds, it's true: Having a sense of presence means being rooted in the present—not being distracted or preoccupied. The two best ways of staying in the moment are (1) being conscious of your breathing and (2) laughing. (That's one reason why audiences love speakers who laugh at themselves and who get them laughing.)
- **Be interested.** If you want others to be interested in what you're saying, you must be interested in it, too. (The best way to be boring—not just momentarily but incessantly—is to be bored.) Be interested in your listeners and how they might be affected by your presentation. Cultivate your sense of curiosity and wonder, and resolve never to talk about something that you don't want to know more about yourself.

- **Be unafraid.** Don't worry about making a fool of yourself. Don't second-guess your every word and gesture. Let your natural enthusiasm and attractiveness shine through.

- **Be connected.** Whether you're speaking to a few people in your office or to a jammed auditorium, build rapport with them. Look them in the eye. Talk to them as if they're your friends. Don't give a speech as much as have a conversation with your audience. Lee Glickstein, founder of Speaking Circles International and an authority on personal magnetism, says, "Speak every word into the eyes and heart of one other person." Think of your presentation as a way of helping them achieve something they value. Let them know how much you care—and they'll care about what you say.

- **Be grounded.** People who project a sense of being in command are not easily swayed or pushed about. They stand their ground. The same is true for powerful speakers. Plant your feet. Imagine that you're rooted to the earth and that its strength flows through you. When you move, do so with a purpose, not just to pace.

Connect with your own passion, connect with the audience, and let them know you want what's good for them, and you won't have to worry about whether you have charisma. You'll have what it takes—whatever it's called—to win an audience's hearts and minds. And that's good enough.

DARE TO BE DIFFERENT

L eaders don't play by the rules. They take risks. They do the unexpected. And when they do that in front of an audience, they catch people unawares. They set themselves apart from the predictable—and predictably boring—mass of other speakers. They make themselves and their message memorable.

Academy Awards acceptance speeches are consistently the most boring and senseless speeches inflicted upon the hapless public. (The president's—any president's—State of the Union Address is a close runner-up.) It's as if every actor, producer, and director at the awards ceremony is working from the same script. Each speech begins with an expression of feigned surprise and quickly devolves into a litany of people to be thanked, a list that goes on almost as long as the credits at the end of a movie. Blah, blah, blah.

Viewers, becoming more and more restless, start to look forward to the commercial breaks. But then, maybe once or twice in the entire and entirely too-long ceremony, someone has the audacity to stand up and say something heartfelt, insightful, surprising. And they shine more brightly than all the other stars.

Most people are, at best, mediocre speakers. And an alarming number of leaders give speeches that closely approximate Muzak—pleasant, painless, and immediately forgotten. Follow their example and no one will pay attention to, care about, or remember anything you say. To make yourself stand out and to make your message memorable, you must be different.

You can do that in two ways: You can say something different. Or you can say it differently.

- **Say something different.**

Why bother saying what your audience already knows and believes or what any other speaker can tell them? Your goal is to change the audience in some way—to change how they see the world or their place in it, to change what they think they're capable of, to change the reasons why they do what they do. So your message can't be the same old same old.

Stake out a position that flies in the face of what people expect to be told. (Instead of "thinking outside the box" or "pushing the envelope," as the clichés go, maybe you should push the box and think outside the envelope.) Say something that cuts across the grain, like "Customers are always wrong." Or "Working more hours than everyone else isn't as much a badge of honor as it is a bad habit." Then defend your position for all you're worth, throwing yourself into the fray with zeal and good cheer. You may surprise your audience by what you end up saying. Who knows, you may even surprise yourself.

To every issue, there's always another side, another point of view, another option. Real leaders look at the same situation as everyone else, but they see something different. They talk about the same things other people talk about, but they say something different.

Richard Nixon left a spotty record as president, but he consistently refused to be predictable. A fierce anti-Communist, he caught the nation and the entire world by surprise when he announced his intention to visit China. Years after leaving office in disgrace, he declined an invitation to address the Republican National Convention, an honor that would have gone a long way in repairing his reputation. When asked why, he said, "People would expect me to endorse the Republican candidate, and leaders can never afford to be predictable."

Socrates did the unpredictable while addressing the jury that had found him guilty of "corrupting the youth." He refused to plead for mercy. Instead, he used his last public discourse to extol the merits of seeking virtue in self-knowledge.

Dwight Eisenhower surprised the nation in his farewell address as president. The former supreme commander of the Allied Forces during the Second World War and a staunch warrior of the Cold War left office warning the nation of the perils of "the military-industrial complex," a term he coined.

Lyndon Johnson shocked the country when, at the end of a prime-time speech about the war in Vietnam, he announced, "I shall not seek, and I will not accept, the nomination of my party for another term as your president."

In politics, business, and community affairs, audiences listen to, respect, and remember leaders who dare to speak the unexpected.

- **Say it differently.**

You may not want or be able to say something new and different. If that's the case, you can at least say it differently.

The executive director of a nonprofit agency was asked to make a short presentation to a convention of other nonprofit leaders. She was told she would have fifteen minutes to explain the main challenges her agency faced and how it was addressing them. What she wasn't told was that four other executive directors would precede her on the same program and each, like her, would speak for fifteen minutes. Each one stood in semidarkness behind the lectern next to a screen where their Power-Point slides took center stage.

By the time she stood to speak, she could sense that the audience was ready for a nap, if not already taking one. She turned off the projector. She asked to have the houselights turned up. She took the microphone in her hand and stepped off the platform into the center aisle.

"I'd like to use my fifteen minutes of fame a little differently," she began. "I'm going to tell you as briefly as possible what my agency does and why we do it. Then I'm going to ask you, based on your experience as leaders in the nonprofit arena and on what you've already heard from the other speakers, to tell me what you think are the challenges my agency faces. And if I can, I'll tell you how we're positioning ourselves to address those challenges."

She worked most of her prepared remarks into her answers to the challenges the audience members posed. They felt engaged. They thought she was brilliant. And they spoke about her speech throughout the rest of the gathering.

Elizabeth Dole did a similar thing in 1996 when she introduced her husband, the Republican candidate for president. "Now, you know tradition is that speakers at the Republican National Convention remain at this very imposing podium," she said. "But tonight I'd like to break with tradition. For two reasons. One, I'm going to be speaking to friends and, secondly, I'm going to be speaking about the man I love and it's just a lot more comfortable for me to do that down here with you." And she strode confidently into the audience with a handheld microphone, talk-show style.

Don't be different just to be different. As a matter of fact, don't even try to be different. Stop, instead, trying to look or sound like everyone else. Be yourself, and if that doesn't make you different, then something is seriously wrong. Just because everyone else in the program or in your organization or in your field uses PowerPoint or stands behind the lectern or sticks to a script doesn't mean you have to.

"'Safety first' has been the motto of the human race for half a million years," wrote turn-of-the-century journalist Herbert N. Casson, "but it has never been the motto of leaders. Leaders must face danger. They must take the risk and blame, and the brunt of the storm."

LEARNING FROM OPRAH

No matter how much of a big shot you may think you are, no matter how high your firm's stock price has soared or how often you're a talking head on CNBC, your audience doesn't *care what you know* until it *knows that you care*.

Caring for an audience—their hopes, goals, and betterment—links all great speakers. Without that caring, you're merely filling a slot on some agenda, and you will never influence or inspire audiences.

Caring about your listeners doesn't necessarily mean you like them, though liking them helps. Caring doesn't even mean you enjoy being around them, though, that too makes speaking to them easier.

Instead, caring about them means wanting what is good for them and using your speech as a way to help them achieve it. The best way to let an audience know you care about them is to show how what you're talking about will help them solve a problem, achieve a goal, or fulfill a need or desire.

Conversely, if you dislike your audience or don't care about their problems, goals, or desires, the solution is simple: *Don't speak to them.* Otherwise, they will sense your antipathy, and you will waste both your listeners' and your own time.

This concern for your audience can't just be philosophical or theo-retical. It must be felt.

Take Oprah Winfrey. She's unique. You can't be like her and probably don't want to be. But when it comes to showing concern for an audience, you can learn a lot from her. Let's look at some of the things she does that you might emulate:

- **Tell your story.** Oprah talks about her impoverished child-hood. (She got her first pair of shoes when she was six. Her par-ents never married, and she was shuttled from her mother to her grandmother to her father.) And she talks about being molested. She does all that—and more—without a hint of self-pity. Because she's fearless about telling her story, she allows others to tell the truth about their lives.
- **Stress what you have in common.** Oprah is one of the world's richest women, yet middle-class, middle-aged women adore her and think of her as "one of us." That's because they identify with the difficult road she's traveled and with her ongoing struggles with weight, relationships, and the demands of a hectic schedule.
- **Listen.** Oprah listens to the experts she brings on her show. She listens—through her staff—to her television audience around the country. And most of all, she listens to the women in her stu-dio audience.
- **Speak conversationally.** Oprah's commencement address at Wellesley College, for example, was as informal and conversational

as any of her TV shows. She spoke in plain language, alternating between run-on sentences and incomplete sentences. She said "I" a lot and "you" almost as often. And when she said "you," she wasn't speaking generically. She was speaking to the people right in front of her.

- **Promote timeless values.** Oprah constantly talks about self-acceptance, forgiveness, compassion, gratitude, and giving back to the community.
- **Acknowledge problems and provide fixes.** Oprah addresses real problems—abused and neglected children, battered women, divorce, cancer, depression—without simplifying their causes or minimizing their severity. But she's never depressing or discouraging, because she's all about finding a fix and making life better.
- **Build community.** Oprah gives an estimated 10 percent of her income to charities. She sponsors and supports philanthropic groups. Her website—www.oprah.com—has dozens and dozens of links to chat and support groups and message boards.

Understand, though, that caring about them doesn't mean everything's lovey-dovey between you and your listeners. You can be mad at them, disappointed by them, even offended by them. You can disagree with them, dislike their way of thinking or acting, and oppose their agenda. As a matter of fact, you might be adamantly at odds with everything they stand for. And your intent may be not to please them but to challenge, confront, and—ultimately—change them totally.

But you can only help them change if you believe that the change you're proposing will benefit them and will improve their welfare. And if *they* believe it, too.

Wanting to shake your audience out of their complacency isn't incompatible with caring. But you need to stir things up in such a way that your listeners embrace your ideas because it's so obvious you really care about them.

How will they *know* you care? Because you're knowledgeable about the subject. Because you took time to understand them, their challenges, hopes, and dreams. You listen to them and treat their suggestions with respect. You argue fairly and intelligently about their problems. And you reward their efforts to change.

For starters, then, you shouldn't even think of taking the lectern without first learning all you can about your listeners, their concerns and situations, their backgrounds and expertise.

Further, make your passion obvious. Engage your audience. "The spirit of the speaker will determine the spirit of the audience," says Roger Ailes, former media consultant for three U.S. presidents and now head of Fox News. So present yourself enthusiastically. Don't speak in a monotone. Instead, show how much you care by expressing your ideas with punch.

Then deal with this issue: If you go in with both guns blazing, won't the audience hate you? Won't that just tick them off and defeat your attempts at changing them? And further, won't such a hostile reception make you so nervous that you give a lousy speech?

Not necessarily.

In fact, you shouldn't give a rip what they think about you. That's irrelevant. So clear your mind of that. (The actress Ashley Judd has an affirmation that she repeats to herself before going onstage or doing an interview. She tells herself, "What other people think of me is none of my business.") Don't stop *caring about them*—instead, stop *caring about what they think*. Care enough to help them with tough love.

In other words, care more about what you're doing (speaking) and what you're speaking about and what your listeners will get from your message than about what others think about you personally.

When you let go of your urge to please or impress others, you can focus on what really matters. You also enjoy what you are doing. As a result, you're more likely to be at the top of your game and to bring all of who you are into what you're doing—that is, helping those you care about.

PART TWO

A NOTEWORTHY EVENT

WHAT ARE YOU GETTING YOURSELF INTO?

It's a leader's responsibility to make not only the speech but the entire event a success. Truth is, if the event bombs, no one will remember how well you spoke or even what you said.

Good judgment, it's sometimes said, comes from bad experience, and a lot of that comes from bad judgment. Here's my horror story: I once got talked into a last-minute gig speaking to a dinner gathering of physicians. I already had a talk that matched the meeting planner's objectives, but I didn't have the time needed to ask questions and prepare for that specific gathering. Bad idea.

So what I didn't learn—until it was too late—was that these docs had been in tedious meetings all day, followed by "social time" with an open bar. After an hour of drinking, the audience sat down to dinner. Each table had open bottles of white and red wine. Three presenters preceded me, each one giving a long, highly technical talk. The wine bottles kept getting emptied and replenished. By the time I was introduced to give my 45-minute talk, "Making Technical Presentations to a Lay Audience," it was 9:45 P.M. You can imagine how that would have gone over if I hadn't made a last-minute decision to radically condense my presentation.

My point, of course, is that you must manage the entire event, not just your remarks. Managing the event has two steps. First, you need to learn as much about the event as possible so you can tailor your message to it. And beyond that, you have to take an active role in shaping the event so it supports your message.

First, know the event. I suggest you spend almost as much time analyzing the event as you do researching your topic. Make it a point to know the room, the host, the audience, the format, the lighting . . . and even whether there are ice cubes in the water pitchers.

Ask—and make sure you get answers to—these questions:

- **Who?** What group is hosting the event? Who's sponsoring it? Who's the meeting planner? How many will be attending? What are their age range, education level, and occupations? What's the ratio of men to women? What do attendees have in common? What's important to them? What are their shared values and their most divisive differences? What do they already know and feel about your topic?
- **What?** What's the nature of the event—a convention, a workshop, a kickoff rally, a celebration, a blow-off-steam conclave? It'll make a difference in what you say and how you say it.
- **When?** When is the event and how long will it be? Where will your speech come within the event? What else is scheduled? Who else is speaking? What immediately precedes and follows your talk?
- **Where?** What's the venue? How's the room set up? Where's

the stage and how's it arranged? Where's the lighting focused? How are the chairs arrayed?

One speaker I know stumbled into this bad setup: The Anaheim Convention Center, site of a meeting with over 20,000 participants, was being renovated. A score of different speakers were giving breakout sessions simultaneously in a hall the size of five airplane hangars, separated only by flimsy curtains. Each speaker tried to talk louder than the others, with the result that no one could think straight, let alone hear anything of value.

• **Why?** Why is the group gathering at this place and time? What do they hope to accomplish? Do they primarily want to learn something or to have a good time? To improve themselves or to connect with peers? To be entertained or to be enlightened?

Every speaker should know the *who, what, when, where,* and *why* of the event where he or she will be speaking. But leaders must do even more. They shouldn't settle for simply knowing the event. They want—or *should* want—to shape it.

As a leader you have more authority and, therefore, more ability to manage the event. You don't have to take what you're given.

Take politicians. Because they speak so often and so much is riding on their image, they're frequently masters at spinning gold from straw.

President George W. Bush's administration is widely considered to have reached new heights in the art of stagecraft. The *New York Times* said Bush's "Top Gun" landing in 2003 on the deck of the carrier USS *Abraham Lincoln* "will be remembered as one of the most audacious moments of presidential theater in American history."

Bush, you may recall, landed on the *Lincoln* aboard an S-3B Viking jet, emerged from the craft in full flight gear, and proceeded to shake hands and hug crew members in front of an array of cameras. Later, he declared "major combat operations in Iraq have ended" in front of a massive "Mission Accomplished" banner. (That his declaration proved to be at least several years premature doesn't detract from the fact that the staging of the event created a powerful message at the time.)

The same team that staged the *Lincoln* event used its magic in almost every other major speech the president gave. They brought in powerful lights to illuminate the Statue of Liberty when he spoke on the anniversary of the 9/11 terrorist attacks. At a speech in Indianapolis promoting his economic plan, they asked men in the crowd behind Mr. Bush to remove their ties so they would look more like the ordinary folk the president said would benefit from his tax cut. And when he spoke in South Dakota, they positioned cameras so the president's profile was perfectly aligned with the profiles on Mount Rushmore.

Of course, you don't have the resources at your command that a president has or the authority to make things happen exactly the way you want. But you have more ability than you think to shape how the event is staged.

PAY ATTENTION TO DETAILS

Depending on how much say you do have in managing the event, pay special attention to these elements.

- **Microphone.** Unless you're going to be standing behind the lectern, ask for a wireless lavaliere microphone. If you're a man wearing a jacket, clip the battery pack on your belt so it can't be seen, thread the wire up your shirt, and clip the mike on your tie. If you're a woman, make sure your outfit allows you to accommodate both the battery pack and the mike. Test the microphone before your speech, preferably before the audience gathers.
- **Stage.** Set the lectern off to the left side of the stage ("downstage right" in theater terms). Leave the center of the stage free to move around in. If you're going to be speaking entirely from the lectern, place it center stage or downstage right. Make sure the lights will always illuminate wherever you're going to be standing. Look at the stage through the eyes of a set designer for a play and do whatever you can to make it enhance your message and goal.
- **Seating.** At the very least, make sure everyone has an unobstructed view of you. Sometimes the seats are bolted in place, and you simply have to work with what you're given. But if possible, have the seats arranged in a fan shape instead of in straight rows so the audience can see more of one another than the backs of other people's heads.
- **Timing.** Even if you can't change the schedule of the event, make sure the audience doesn't have to sit through any more than 20 minutes of preliminary remarks or of other speeches before you speak.

Remember, you can always say no. If the event is shaping up to be something you don't want to participate in, if it won't allow you to make the impact you want your message to have, or if it runs counter in spirit or in tone to how you want to be known, disengage. Some speak from experience; others, from experience, don't speak.

So as gracefully as possible, bow out. Because you're a leader, other opportunities and better engagements will surely come.

Don't Speak Unless You
Can Do Some Good

L eaders, like novelists, have at best only a few big things to say. Wisdom consists in not saying them *ad nauseam*.

As a leader you're a spokesperson for your organization, whether it's a multinational corporation or a one-person operation. And by necessity, you speak a lot—to win the public's notice and goodwill or to shape their perceptions, to rally the troops, to attract clients or customers, to keep your funding sources informed and happy. But when you speak too often, you risk becoming repetitious. Then you lose your audience's interest and respect, and you cheapen your message.

Abraham Lincoln campaigned tirelessly for the Republican nomination for president in 1860. He spoke daily and at great length, frequently debating his opponent, Stephen Douglas, for two to three hours at a time.

But Lincoln stopped speaking once he won the nomination. And even after winning the presidency, he made no formal speech for the five months between the election and his inauguration. Though he spoke off-the-cuff and briefly at every stop along his train's route from Illinois to Washington, he gave no formal talk.

The result? His inaugural address got everyone's attention. His conciliatory remarks were published and commented upon in newspapers in both the North and the South.

Similarly, Calvin Coolidge refrained from speaking so much that he earned the nickname "Silent Cal" and gained a reputation for always being worth listening to. "The words of the President have an enormous weight," he wrote in his autobiography, "and ought not to be used indiscriminately."

The same could be said about any leader. If you take to the platform too frequently (or for too long), you will bore your audience, lose your celebrity status, and lessen your impact. And you probably will have trouble getting your other work done.

WHEN TO SAY NO

Other reasons—besides wanting to avoid sounding repetitious—exist for declining an invitation to speak:

- **You're the wrong person.** Maybe you and what you represent don't match the needs of the gathering. Perhaps you and the audience would be better served if you sent your CFO, director of human resources, or public information officer to take up the cudgel. If other people can represent your group and advance its objectives as well as you can, let them.

- **It's the wrong audience.** Does this group have an investment in your organization's mission or activities? Can it influence your success? If not, you gain little by speaking to them. (And they have equally little to gain from listening to you.) As a leader, you should speak only to audiences that will do something with your speech—talk it up, publish it, denounce it, act on it, dissect it, recoil in horror . . . something.

- **It's the wrong event.** If the purpose or "energy" of the event runs counter to your message or if the event is poorly planned and lacks heft, avoid it. You don't want to trivialize your big ideas by speaking to a gathering thrown together at the last minute or for the wrong reason.

To be avoided: Speaking before a group that has no clearly stated reason for gathering, that has no interest in your message, or that's just received bad news (unless you're directly addressing that event). A case in point: A speaker was hired to give a talk on teamwork at a high-tech firm's annual retreat. When she checked in with the meeting planner an hour before her presentation, she found out that half the attendees had just been informed they were being "downsized." Could the speaker, the planner asked, work something about motivation into her talk? Ouch!

- **It's the wrong venue.** You should put as much thought into where you're speaking—the location, setup, and ambience—as you put into what you wear. You can't demand that Elizabethan-garbed trumpeters herald your entrance. But you can—and should—refuse to speak in the crowded, overheated ballroom of a cheap hotel where the clamor from the kitchen or an adjoining clown convention would be enough to drown out a drill sergeant.

- **It's the wrong time.** Avoid, if at all possible, speaking in the afternoon slump—1:30 P.M. to 2:30 P.M. And try not to speak late in the evening after a speech-weary audience has sated itself on a heavy meal and an open bar. And don't speak too soon after a tragedy, a corporate upheaval, or some other unsettling event, unless you are addressing that occurrence.

Even if you are the right person and everything else is right, you still might be better off choosing not to speak. In one case, a new president began routinely dropping in on the quarterly meetings of her West Coast operation, where she felt obliged to speak at each event. At first, her audience was honored. The employees appreciated hearing her ideas about the company and its future. But after a year—and four speeches covering much the same ground—even she began to lose interest in what she was saying.

So for the next three quarterly meetings, she simply sat in the audience and listened to what others had to say. Finally, when she rose to speak a year after having last spoken, the employees were once again eager to hear her.

People tend to discount whatever is plentiful and readily available. So parcel out your thoughts carefully. Speak less often and have a bigger impact.

WHO ARE THESE GUYS?

A motivational speaker complained that she often got a mixed response to her speeches. Some audiences cheered and cried for more; others sat passive and unappreciative. "Why the difference?" she asked me. "I'm good, and I give my best, no matter which group I'm speaking to."

So to give her feedback, I went to observe one of her talks. In a keynote speech titled "The Joys of Marriage," she told wonderful stories and offered homey wisdom and advice culled from her experience as a marriage counselor and from her own twenty-seven years of marriage. And she was right, she *was* good. In fact, she was terrific. She spoke without notes, had impeccable timing, and was warm and immensely likable, with a self-deprecating Erma Bombeck–like wit. But the longer she spoke, the icier the audience became.

I couldn't understand why until I looked at the pamphlet handed out at the door. The conference, titled "New Beginnings," was sponsored by NACSDC, which I learned from reading the small print was the North American Conference of Separated and Divorced Catholics. No wonder the audience members looked as if they wanted to lynch her.

It turns out this speaker rarely, if ever, asked anything about the audience she was about to address. Sounding a bit defensive, she told me, "I believe that the themes of my speech are universal."

Well, la-*de*-da. She and her audience weren't on the same page; in fact, they weren't even in the same library. No number of finely wrought phrases, perfectly polished anecdotes, or smoother-than-silk delivery techniques will make up for blindly giving the totally wrong speech to the wrong audience. You must know to whom you're speaking.

Do you remember that scene from the movie *Butch Cassidy and the Sundance Kid* in which Butch and Sundance are chased by a ridiculously determined posse? The two outlaws ride up mountains, over rocks, through deserts, across streams, hour after hour, mile after mile—and *still* they see the plume of dust from their pursuers doggedly tracking them no matter what they do or which way they turn.

Finally, Sundance turns to Butch in frustration and asks, "Who *are* these guys?" Speakers would do well to ask the same question *before* they speak.

Don't be clueless about your audience's needs and expectations. Don't be, for instance, like the financial planner who spoke passionately about building a nest egg for retirement . . . to a Kiwanis Club whose members were well into their seventies and eighties. Don't emulate the humorist who spoke—without irony—about the need to inject fun and frivolity into every workplace conversation . . . to a group of funeral directors.

Those are big, obvious goofs. But more often than not, what a speaker is ignorant about are the small things, like preferred terminology. Such blind spots lead the audience to question the speaker's credibility or depth of concern. After all, the listeners think, "If you don't know the basics, what *else* don't you know?" Or, "If you don't care enough about us to learn even a little about us, how sincere can you really be?"

For example, one expert in customer retention met resistance from an audience of savings and loan officers because she kept referring to the audience's "customers." Only later did she learn that S&Ls have "members," not customers. A tiny miscue? Perhaps. But it loomed large for the audience that was paying this "expert" to give them advice.

Like a conversation, a speech isn't just about what you know or how you say it. It's about what the audience *hears, understands, feels, needs*, and—ultimately—*takes away* from your speech. A good chunk of your preparation time should be spent analyzing your audience. In fact, it's probably impossible to do too much research into who your listeners are.

Of course, sometimes what you find out about your audience will make you—or *should* make you—question why you're even speaking to them.

Here are the most common questions to ask about your listeners before speaking to them:

1. Who, exactly, are they? How many will be in the audience? What's their profession, business, or work? What positions do they hold? What's their educational and economic background? What's the age range and the ratio of men to women? What do they have in common?

2. How knowledgeable are they? What do they already know about your topic? How much will you have to explain to them and at what level of detail? Do they know your jargon and acronyms, or should you avoid those terms? (Usually, it's smart to avoid them anyway, or at least to explain them briefly the first time you use them.) And do you know *their* jargon and acronyms?

3. What do they already feel about your topic? Are they completely on your side or hostile to your position? It's not always easy or pleasant to speak to people who are dead set against what you're proposing, but sometimes it's necessary. And in any case, it helps to know in advance what you're facing.

I divide audience members into five kinds: (1) advocates, (2) supporters, (3) neutrals, (4) naysayers, and 5) opponents. Generally speaking, you can at best move people one or two steps higher on the scale. You might as well try to sell stethoscopes to tree surgeons as try to turn opponents into advocates. (It can be done, but it's rarely accomplished in a single speech.) You might, however, be able to turn opponents who would actively campaign against your plan into neutrals who won't oppose you.

4. What are their most pressing concerns or fears? If your research can uncover your listeners' bugaboos, you can either address them or maneuver around them.

5. What's their style of learning? How do they prefer being presented to? Are they expecting you to give a formal presentation with time at the end reserved for Q&A? Do they want you to be informal, sitting around a conference table and taking their questions throughout your presentation? Do they want handouts and lots of collateral material? Do they see themselves as passive recipients of what you have to say or as active participants, shaping the direction and format of the presentation?

6. What shouldn't you talk about? Audiences often have sore spots, painful recent memories, or secrets that everyone knows but doesn't talk about. These are hard to discover. Because no one wants to mention them, they may not tell you about them when you ask. But if you're sensitive, you might be able to sniff out the forbidden topics and save yourself a lot of heartache by avoiding them. Even if you're the type of person who enjoys kicking other people's sacred cows, you'd be better off at least knowing in advance that you'll be doing so.

SPEAKING TO A FOREIGN AUDIENCE

When speaking internationally, you have to take into account yet another level of complexity in analyzing your audience—cultural differences and sensitivities.

In China, for example, you don't want to talk about Taiwan or use the number four, which connotes death and is considered unlucky. The Japanese tend to close their eyes and nod their heads slightly during a presentation to show concentration and attentiveness. (They also do it when they're tired or bored.) The Australians, the Irish, and the English enjoy humor in a speech, while the Germans and the French often consider it frivolous. People from South and Central America want speakers from the United States to call themselves "North Americans," not "Americans." And so on.

So if you're going to be speaking abroad, you need to take the following extra steps:

• **Seek extra background.** Speak to your host. Explain your desire to avoid giving offense, and ask for help in understanding local customs. Consult books and websites that give specific advice about the country you'll be visiting.

- **Avoid jargon, slang, and idioms.** Although people in other countries are often surprisingly well versed about what's happening in the United States—at least about our politics, celebrities, and entertainment—it's best not to assume they know current figures of speech.
- **Abbreviate your speech.** Cut down on how much material you plan to present. It's always better to quit speaking before your audience quits listening.
- **Speak slowly and clearly.** Even foreign listeners conversant in English will appreciate the courtesy you show by speaking less rapidly and more clearly.
- **Work with translators.** If your speech is going to be translated, give the translator a written copy as far in advance as possible. Meet with him or her to review difficult words or concepts.

Making the effort to learn all you can about your listeners is one of the hallmarks of a leader. Or as the actor Jimmy Stewart put it, "Never treat your audience as customers, always as partners."

THE ETERNAL
QUESTION: WIIFM?

WIIFM?—*What's in It for Me?*—is the radio station we all play quietly in the back of our minds. And it's the one that leaders need to tune in to when they're figuring out how to get their audience to do what the speaker wants.

Simply telling audiences what to think, feel, or do—ordering them about—doesn't work anymore, if it ever did. Anyone who thinks higher-ups still decide and the worker bees automatically "Just do it!" has never tried to switch the kind of snacks sold in the employee lounge, let alone initiate some major change.

So as you're giving your speech, your listeners are always asking themselves WIIFM? They're assessing how what you're saying affects them—either positively or negatively. If they can't figure it out, they'll stop listening. (If you've got enough authority or if they're feeling polite, they may *look* as though they're listening. But they're not.)

WIIFM isn't just a self-centered, egotistical, or narcissistic question. (Probably even saints ask it.) Because it's totally natural for anybody to ask: How will this affect me? What benefits will I receive? Why should I care? How will it support my values or concerns?

Oddly, though, some leaders just don't get it. I recall one boss at a medical-device firm whose department had wildly surpassed its goals for the previous year. He wanted to inspire the troops to keep up their hard work and long hours so the department would exceed even higher quotas set for the current year.

He gathered the rank and file for what he termed a pep rally. Arranging them in front of a window overlooking the parking lot, he pointed to a new, midnight-blue Porsche 911. "See that car there? The bonus I got because we did so well last year helped pay for that beauty," he said. "Now my wife wants one. So I know I can trust you all to keep up your hard work."

You can imagine how fired-up his audience was after that.

Every speech needs an objective. And this leader's objective was fine: Inspire the staff to meet or exceed the new goals. But his approach was stupid: Work longer and harder so I can buy my wife an expensive new sports car.

If, instead, he'd asked WIIFM?, he might have said something like this:

We exceeded last year's goals. Congratulations! *[Praise their hard work and success. Make them feel good about it.]* I hope you all enjoyed your well-deserved bonuses. I know I enjoyed mine. I used it to make a down payment on a car I've always dreamed about. I know some of you have used your bonuses to pursue your own dreams. Now I'm asking you to keep up the good work, to redouble your efforts. So maybe this time next year we'll be celebrating again. And maybe we'll be enjoying another great bonus and realizing yet another piece of our dreams.

Of course, this approach would only work if everyone benefited from their hard work. If the boss was the only one who got a bonus, he'd be wiser saying nothing at all. In fact, if that's the case, he should probably refrain from standing too close to a window when he's showing off his shiny, new Porsche to his overworked and underremunerated employees.

It's perfectly legitimate as a leader to have your own objective, what *you* want to accomplish. And it's legitimate to tell the audience what you want them to think, feel, or do. But it's important to understand that audiences have their own objectives, which may or may not coincide with yours. So you need to figure out why *they* would want to think, feel, or do what you want them to.

In other words, you must discover the audience's motivation, their reason for wanting what you want. When I'm preparing a speech, whether for myself or for someone else, I find this question—Why would the audience want what I want?—to be the hardest, most time-consuming one to answer. But if I can't answer it, I don't have a speech.

Do you want the audience to donate to your charity? To walk precincts for your candidate? To give the green light to your project? To use your services? To support your initiative? To fund your start-up? Great. Now all you have to do is to figure out why they would want to.

And the easiest way to appeal to what your listeners want—in other words, to answer their WIIFM? question—is to show how they can use your idea or proposal to . . .

- **Solve a problem of theirs.** Show them how your proposal or idea will rid them of something they don't want, fix something that's not working, get them out of a bad situation, save them time or money, or make a difficult or complex task easier.

- **Achieve a goal of theirs.** Tell them how they can gain something they desire (such as money, time, or recognition) or accomplish a task that's important to them (maybe improve their health, learn a skill, or win a promotion).

- **Satisfy a need of theirs.** Explain how acting in a certain way would be in alignment with or advance their values, desires, or dreams (perhaps show they're highly ethical, generous, or community-minded).

It's your call, really, whether you want to talk in terms of solving problems, achieving goals, or satisfying needs. They're all overlapping aspects of the same concept.

A SAR STORY

One way to show your audience how they will benefit from your proposal is to use what is sometimes called a SAR story. SAR stands for situation, action, result. It's a variation of a format salespeople often use, but it works equally well for problem-solving or goal-achieving speeches.

- **Situation.** Describe a real person who was in a situation similar to one that the people in your audience are in. Show how that person was negatively affected by a problem, an unmet goal, or an unfulfilled need. Be specific and concrete. You want your audience members to say to themselves, "Yeah, I'm in that same kind of bind. And I don't like it."

- **Action.** Show how that person adopted your idea, mindset, proposal, product, or service and, in doing so, solved the problem, achieved the goal, or satisfied the need.

- **Result.** Show the positive outcome that the person realized as a consequence of taking the action.

Audiences, of course, are made up of diverse individuals so there's no *one* motivator that will apply to everyone. Thus, you'll do well to touch on a number of different reasons why your audience would want what you want.

All this effort to dovetail your listeners' aims with yours hinges on two basic assumptions: First, you have the audience's best interests at heart. And second, you understand your audience well enough to know what motivates them. And as a leader, you *do*, don't you?

PART THREE

A COMPELLING MESSAGE

CONTENT IS KING

Trainers and "presentation experts" never tire of claiming that only 7 percent of a speech's meaning is communicated by the words you speak. Thirty-eight percent, or so the story goes, is conveyed through your vocal tone and a whopping 55 percent by your body language.

The implication is clear: What you say isn't nearly as important as how you say it. Delivery trumps content.

Nonsense! That idiotic claim comes from a misreading of a small group of studies done by a psychology professor more than forty years ago, studies about interpersonal communications that had a very limited scope. When those "conclusions" are (mis)applied to making a speech, they're so clearly wrongheaded that anyone giving the matter a few seconds of thought would be too embarrassed to repeat them.

If your voice and body language express 93 percent of what you mean, why bother preparing a speech that articulates what you believe and resonates with what your audience longs to hear? Why not just stand in front of the audience and say whatever comes to mind? As long as you use the right tone of voice and the right gestures, the audience will understand what you mean. At least, they'll get 93 percent of it, which is good enough. Right?

Wrong.

It's true that some perfectly good ideas have been ignored or dis-counted because they were poorly delivered. And, conversely, some bogus ideas have made more of an impact than they deserve because they were so well delivered. So I'm not saying that delivery is unimportant. Far from it. A masterful delivery is one of the cornerstones of a great speech.

But clearly the words you use and what they mean are more impor-tant than how you say them. Content is king. Delivery is merely its help-ful, or unhelpful, servant.

When my clients need to spruce up their appearance, I refer them to an image consultant I know. She's accustomed to working with business professionals, so she doesn't go for glamour or glitz. "I don't want people to look at someone I've dressed and say, 'That's a great tie' or 'I love that blouse,'" she explains. "I want them to say, 'You look sharp.'"

Similarly, you don't want people to go away from your speech saying, "You used great vocal variety" or "Your gestures were truly outstanding." Instead, you want them to get the big picture. You want them to see things the way you see things, to feel about them the way you feel about them, to act the way you want them to act. You want people to pay at-tention *to your message*, to remember it, and to be changed by it.

Three elements compose a compelling message: a big idea, a clear structure, and telling words.

Idea. Each speech should lay out one, and only one, idea. But it's got to be a big idea—big in scope or insight or implication, big enough to jus-tify talking about it, big enough to engage the audience's full attention.

Structure. The structure of your speech—how it's organized, how its pieces fit together—is like the blueprint for a house. It's the framework on which you build your message piece by piece. It has to be simple because audiences today aren't sophisticated listeners. (They're skilled visual observers and accomplished multitaskers, but that's another thing altogether.) If the underlying structure is weak or faulty, your speech will fall apart under its own weight or be blown over by the weakest wind of disagreement.

Words. The words you choose can either clarify your message or confuse it, strengthen it or undercut it. Vigorous speaking is concise. Your speech, to apply Strunk's and White's advice in *The Elements of Style* to speaking, "should contain no unnecessary words or sentences, for the same reason that a drawing should have no unnecessary lines and a machine no unnecessary parts. This doesn't mean that you must make all your sentences short or that you avoid all detail. But it does mean that you make every word count." Build your speech around nouns and active verbs. When given the choice between longer, more impressive-sounding words and shorter, more concrete ones, choose the latter.

SPOKEN WORDS

Understanding the difference between spoken words and written words can help you prepare better speeches.

- Spoken words require more attention to sound. For instance, you probably would never say "eschew" from the podium—it sounds too stuffy—but you could use it in a written piece. Some word combinations—fluent French, for example, or bright blue—can be difficult to pronounce, especially when you are nervous and your mouth is dry. (That's one reason it's always wise to practice your speeches out loud: to discover—and revise—sounds that might give you trouble before you're in front of a crowd.)

- Spoken words need to be conversational. You can get away with more formal usage when you're writing. But when you're giving a talk, people expect you to sound somewhat as you sound when you're speaking to them in a conversation.

- Spoken words must be immediately—or almost immediately—understood. If you use a word in writing that readers don't understand, they can think about it for a moment, try to figure it out from the context, or perhaps look it up, then resume reading. But if you use a word that listeners don't understand, they stop listening to you to figure it out. They stop listening; you keep speaking. When they figure it out—if they do—they tune back in to what you're saying only to find that they've missed something.

Here are five rhetorical devices you can easily use to give your speeches more power and to make them more memorable without fear of sounding like an old-fashioned orator.

- **The rule of three:** Link together three elements—words, phrases, or sentences—that are parallel in form and you make a memorable combination. "I stand before you today the representative of a family in grief, in a country in mourning, before a world in shock" (Lord Spencer at the funeral of his sister, Princess Diana).

• **Repetition:** When you want your words to have the greatest impact, repeat them. You can repeat an entire sentence—just one sentence per speech—as long at it's your main point and it's well crafted. "I have a dream" (Martin Luther King). Or you can repeat a single word or phrase throughout a longer section. "My Republican Party today—it is not a conservative party. *It is soft on* globalism. *It is soft on* big government. *It is soft on* the Second Amendment. *It is soft on* life" (Patrick Buchanan).

• **Not this, but that:** One of the best ways to clarify a point and make it memorable is to contrast it with something else. State what it isn't first, followed immediately by what it is. "September 11th was not an isolated event, but a tragic prologue" (Tony Blair). "We are here not to see through one another, but to see one another through" (Anne Lamott).

• **It's like:** Whether you say something is *like* something else (simile) or *is* something else (metaphor), you're making a powerful comparison. "This [hearing] is a circus. It's a national disgrace. And from my standpoint, as a black American, it is a high-tech lynching for uppity blacks who in any way deign to think for themselves" (Clarence Thomas).

• **Rhetorical question:** By asking a question that implies its own answer, you're prompting the audience to arrive at the same conclusion as you. "Can anyone look at the record of this Administration and say, 'Well done'? Can anyone compare the state of our economy when the Carter Administration took office with where we are today and say, 'Keep up the good work'? Can anyone look at our reduced standing in the world today and say, 'Let's have four more years of this'?" (Ronald Reagan).

Words and content matter because a good speech is like good literature. "A speech is poetry: cadence, rhythm, imagery, sweep," says celebrated Reagan speechwriter Peggy Noonan. "A speech reminds us that words, like children, have the power to make dance the dullest beanbag of a heart."

WHAT'S THE BIG IDEA?

I f you're a Hollywood writer lucky enough to get in front of producers, you might get 15 seconds of their divided attention to pitch the concept for your script. That's not only because Hollywood producers are busy, self-involved moguls with the attention span of a gnat. It's also because they know that a good movie tells *one simple, powerful story*. If you can't sum it up in a sentence or two, it's not a good story—and it won't make a good movie.

The same is true for a speech. A movie tells one story. A speech develops one idea. But it's got to be a *good* idea—a policy, a direction, an insight, a prescription. Something that provides clarity and meaning, something that's both intellectually and emotionally engaging. It's got to be what I call a Big Idea.

Some recent examples of Big Ideas:

- Al Gore's *An Inconvenient Truth:* "Global warming isn't just a political issue, it's the biggest moral challenge facing our world."
- Kathy Cloninger, CEO of the Girl Scouts of the USA: "Overwhelming research and nearly a century of experience in Girl Scouting show that, in an all-girl environment, girls feel much freer to try, to fail, to succeed, and to express themselves and their dreams."

- Bill Gates's commencement speech at Harvard: "Humanity's greatest advances are not in its discoveries—but in how those discoveries are applied to reduce inequity."
- Randy Pausch, professor of computer science, giving *the professor's last lecture:* "Brick walls are there for a reason: they let us prove how badly we want things."

A speech articulating your single Big Idea can have as many as three to five main points. (Three is better than five, and—don't ask me why—odd numbers seem to work better than even.)

For example, your Big Idea may be *"We have to stop doing business as usual."* That's the message you want to leave your audience with. But your main points might explain (1) why business as usual isn't working the way it used to, (2) how you want business to change, and (3) what it's going to look like when it is changed.

Or your idea may be *"The project we've just completed symbolizes what's best about our company."* You could then talk about (1) the scope of the project, (2) the reasons it was so successful, and (3) why it represents the company at its best.

Whittling down your message to one Big Idea takes discipline. Early in his military career Dwight Eisenhower drafted speeches for General Douglas MacArthur. He told other speechwriters, "If you can't put the bottom-line message on the inside of a matchbook, you're not doing your job." (I tell clients to write the idea for their speech on the backside of their business card.)

MAKE IT MEMORABLE

Masterful speakers use a common rhetorical device to alert their audiences to their Big Idea. It has three steps: (1) the setup, (2) a pause, and (3) the punch line. (The punch line is your one-sentence Big Idea.) This technique is the speaker's equivalent of italicizing or underlining. You can only use it once in every speech.

For example:

- "And so my fellow Americans [pause] ask not what your country can do for you—ask what you can do for your country" (John F. Kennedy).
- "Let me again assert my firm belief that [pause] the only thing we have to fear is fear itself" (Franklin Roosevelt).
- "Believe one thing if nothing else, [pause] I did what I thought was right for our country" (Tony Blair).

Here are some setups you might try:

- "There's one thing I want to leave you with, and it's this [pause] . . ."
- "If you take only one idea from my speech, remember this [pause] . . ."
- "What I want to say and what I need you to know is this [pause] . . ."

There is, of course, a downside to stating your idea so clearly and succinctly that you can write it on a business card: If it's a stupid, insipid, or anemic idea, people will know it for what it's worth. Or for what it's not worth.

Bad speeches usually suffer from one of three problems: a small idea hiding behind big words, mere information instead of ideas, or too many ideas.

Small ideas/Big words. Many speakers confuse using big words—jargon, buzzwords, and corporate-speak—with presenting a big idea. An executive once sent me the rough draft of a speech he'd been working on and asked me to clean it up. I replaced words and phrases that didn't mean much, doing the best I could to clarify what he was saying in plain and (I hoped) elegant English. "But when I say it that way," he complained, "there's not much substance to it." He said it, not me.

If you hear a speaker say something like "At the end of the day, going forward we'll have to reengineer our operational priorities to optimize our mission-critical architecture to provide value add to our stakeholders," don't be taken in by it. In my experience, the bigger the words speakers use, the smaller the ideas they advocate.

Information instead of ideas. People who are accustomed to giving technical briefings often assemble as much information as possible and import it willy-nilly into PowerPoint. They don't organize it into a cohesive, meaningful whole. Why bother? PowerPoint lets you call up a blank slide, fill it in, and go on to the next. You can create any number of slides—*hundreds,* if you like—without ever tying anything together into a coherent or compelling idea.

As a speaker, begin by sifting through the pertinent information, picking out what's valuable, and discarding the rest. Then tie it all together in a way that makes sense of it. Write out your one organizing principle or thought—your Big Idea. Then structure the information you've assmbled to supporrt your idea. Use only as much information as you need to prove or illustrate your main idea. (Then ask yourself if using PowerPoint would help make your points.)

Too many ideas. Inexperienced speakers present too many ideas because they fear appearing stupid or running out of things to say before their time is up. They don't realize that presenting too many ideas is almost as bad as presenting none at all.

There are three variations of a speech that presents too many ideas:

1. The Whac-a-Mole speech. The speaker raises an idea, seemingly at random, and rants about it before raising another and ranting some more. (For the uninitiated, Whac-a-Mole in an arcade game that consists of a waist-high console with holes on top. When a mole pops up from one of the holes, the player pounds it with a mallet. Each time a mole is beaten down, others pop up.) When this type of speech is over, audiences feel bludgeoned into submission.

2. The rice-at-a-wedding speech. The speaker tosses numerous ideas in the general direction of the audience in a gesture of goodwill, not knowing the meaning of the custom but hoping that something worthwhile sticks. While hardly effective, this type of speech—if it doesn't go on too long—leaves audiences feeling good in a vague sort of way.

3. The shotgun speech. The speaker shoots as many ideas as possible in the general direction of the audience in the hope that some idea will hit the target. Audiences go away feeling puzzled.

It takes moxie to state your idea baldly. But that's what being a real leader is all about—saying what you mean in a way that people can't misconstrue or second-guess. Winston Churchill put it this way: "When you have an important point to make, don't try to be subtle or clever. Use a pile driver. Hit the point once. Then come back and hit it again. Then hit it a third time—a tremendous whack."

NO SPEECH OVER 20 MINUTES

While no terminally ill patient has ever said, "I wish I'd spent more time at the office," neither has any leader been known to utter, "Boy, I wish I'd spoken longer." When is the last time *you* wanted a speaker to talk longer?

In fact, well-focused brevity is the hallmark of a good speech. The most notable speeches in history have been short ones. For instance:

- Patrick Henry's "Give me liberty or give me death" speech before the Virginia House of Burgesses lasted 6 minutes.
- Lincoln's Gettysburg Address took 2 minutes.
- Franklin Roosevelt's address to the nation after Pearl Harbor was over in 7 minutes.
- Martin Luther King Jr.'s famous "I Have a Dream" speech took 16 minutes.
- Ronald Reagan's response to the Space Shuttle Challenger tragedy (". . . touched the face of God") was 4½ minutes.
- And Margaret Thatcher's moving tribute to Reagan ("We have lost a great president, a great American and a great man. And I have lost a dear friend") was just 7 minutes long.

"If you cannot say what you have to say in twenty minutes," Lord Brabazon, the pioneering British aviator, said, "you should go away and write a book about it." And *brevity* was the first rule of speaking as espoused by Theodore Sorensen, John F. Kennedy's celebrated speechwriter. (Levity, charity, and clarity were his other rules.) But why, really, is short better?

Well, for one thing, a short speech is likely to be more focused. Lincoln is reputed to have said that if he was asked to give a two-hour speech, he could do so almost immediately. But for a two-minute speech, he'd need days or weeks to get ready.

A related reason is that a short speech has less chance of boring an audience. If you know what you want to say and have planned how to say it, you're more likely to plant one clear idea in the minds of the audience without allowing extra time for daydreaming or checking for cellphone messages.

Also, in this age of PDAs, instant messaging, and other electronic distractions, audiences don't have the attention spans they may have once had. What's more, you want to leave your audience wanting more of you, not less.

KEEP IT SHORT AND SIMPLE

One of the best ways to improve a speech is to make it simpler . . . and simpler usually implies shorter. Simplifying a speech makes it easier for you to deliver and easier for your audience to understand and remember.

Paradoxically, simplifying your speech is all the more important when you're dealing with sophisticated, complex material.

Here are five ways to simplify your message:

1. Limit your focus. Beginners want to impress their audiences with how much they know so they say everything. Leaders, secure in their authority, focus on what matters most. They limit the scope of their speech to fit the time available and the learning style of the audience.

2. Eliminate the nonessential. Dive right into what you want to say and what your listeners need to know. That means dropping the opening pleasantries ("I'm happy to be here with you today"), side issues ("This isn't really related to the subject, but . . ."), and what everyone already knows ("Wow, you're here from all over the country and . . .").

3. Group-related material. When preparing, once you've listed everything you think the audience needs to know and feel about your proposal, put similar items together. For instance, instead of talking about "The Twenty-one Things You Need to Know About Insomnia," build your speech around the causes of insomnia, its effects, and its treatment or cures.

4. Let the audience decide. Outline the most important issues and explain them briefly. Then take the listeners' questions. Let them determine what they want to know more about.

5. Repeat. Any point that's worth making is worth repeating. Audiences often are distracted, overworked, and overwhelmed. So make your main points, then repeat them. You don't need to say them exactly the same way each time, but even if you do, people won't mind because, in all likelihood, they probably won't even notice.

To pare your speech to twenty minutes or less, be sure to:

Start with the main course. Jettison the formalities. Don't thank the emcee, don't acknowledge the other dignitaries present, don't apologize or waste time explaining how or why your time is limited. Don't explain how you thought of the idea, unless that's part of what you're talking about. Just *begin*.

Develop one idea. Make it sharp and to the point. And make it a strong idea, because you're not going to be able to hide beneath a surfeit of words. In fact, you want to eliminate all nonessential words, phrases, sentences. (The Gettysburg Address had 272 words. Lincoln was preceded that day by Edward Everett, whose talk contained 13,607 words. Which one do you remember?)

Revise, revise, revise. Eliminate asides and tangents. Put bloated expressions on a diet. (Why say "at that point in time" when "then" will suffice?) Of all the evidence you can muster to support or substantiate your main point, present only as much as your audience needs to know in order to agree with you. (Keep the other evidence on hand to use during the Q&A, if you get the chance.) "What information consumes is rather obvious: It consumes the attention of its recipients," said Herbert Simon, recipient of the Nobel Memorial Prize in Economics. "Hence, a wealth of information creates a poverty of attention."

Finish before your assigned time is up. Leave at the height of the party and have the audience begging for more. As Ellen DeGeneres said when hosting the Oscars, "It's not that we don't have time for long speeches. We don't have time for boring speeches."

Once you've said "in conclusion" or "finally" or anything else that leads the audience to believe you're winding down, you have, at most, one minute to wrap it up. So never introduce new material in your conclusion. To do so will make your listeners feel as if they're on a plane that's making its final approach—after they've dutifully stowed their personal belongings, fastened their seat belts, and raised their trays to the full, upright position—only to have the pilot tell them he's going to pull out of the descent and circle the airport a few more times.

Leaders stand up for what they believe and, having said it, they sit down. Get in. Get real. Get out.

START RIGHT

In speechmaking, as in skydiving, the scariest part comes at the beginning. That's true for both the speaker and the audience.

For the first minute or so of any talk, you're fighting off an anxiety attack. And your listeners are waging an inner conflict of their own, hoping that you'll make good use of their time but fearing that you'll be as irrelevant as most other speakers they've heard. They're asking themselves, "Did I make a big mistake in coming to hear this person instead of getting more work done or staying home and watching a repeat of *American Idol*?"

Depending on the overall length of your speech, your introduction can be as short as 15 seconds or as long as 5 minutes. In that time it has to accomplish three objectives: (1) to get the audience's attention, (2) to introduce yourself, and (3) to give an overview of the speech.

Before doing anything else, you have to break through the audience's preoccupation. If you're speaking at the beginning of the program, they are probably still settling in. They're making themselves comfortable and checking out the room, the people around them, and anything else that grabs their attention. If you're speaking later on, they may be fidgeting, bored by what preceded you or needing to take a bathroom break. They're busy. They're tired. And they're multi-taskers with a limited ability to focus on any one thing or any one person for any length of time. Even if they're sitting quietly, looking attentive, imagine that they're inwardly a bunch of kindergartners on a sugar high, running around wildly and screaming. It's up to you to make yourself seen and heard, to say in effect, "Hey, over here. Look at me. Listen up."

Next, you have to introduce yourself. The formal introduction that someone else read before you began speaking lets people know something about you, your experience and qualifications. Now it's time to let them meet *you* face-to-face. The first thing they're going to do is look you over. They'll make judgments based on what you're wearing, how you're groomed, and how you carry yourself. (They've been doing this, by the way, from the moment they first laid eyes on you. If you're sitting on the stage or in the front row or even if you're standing in the wings, as long as the audience can see you, consider yourself on.) Then they'll listen to the sound of your voice, its tone and pitch, its pacing, and what kind of accent you have. Finally, they'll tune in to what you're actually saying. All the while, your listeners are asking themselves if they like you, if they trust you, if they respect you. Most audiences will answer those questions for themselves within the first 30 seconds. If they answer in the negative, you really, *really* have your work cut out for you.

The third thing your introduction needs to do is give an overview of your speech. Introduce your Big Idea. (When Bono, the lead singer for U2 and outspoken human rights advocate, addressed the NAACP, his big idea was "We need the community that taught the world about civil rights to teach it about human rights.") Let people know what to expect—what you're talking about and how you're going to talk about it. As the dictum goes, tell people what you're going to tell them.

Here's what *not* to do:

- **Don't start with a joke.** Unless you're a gifted comic, this invites disaster. On the other hand, making some humorous, mildly self-deprecating remark is a great way to begin. For instance, in 2008 presidential aspirant Senator John McCain often told audiences, "I'm older than dirt and have got more scars than Frankenstein" as a way to deflect questions about his age (seventy-one) and the vestiges of skin-cancer surgery on his face.

- **Don't waste time on pleasantries.** Don't tell your listeners how happy you are to be speaking to them. Don't tell them what a great group they appear to be. Don't acknowledge dignitaries in the audience. That's all hooey that squanders the force of your opening. In other words, don't introduce your introduction. (It may be appropriate to say something about your audience or about dignitaries later in your speech, when doing so won't sound like you're kissing up to them.)

- **Don't apologize.** Don't say that you're sorry you didn't have sufficient time to prepare or that you're not a better speaker or that you're nervous. Don't put yourself and your insecurities up front. You're insulting the audience—and yourself—if you do that. Instead, focus on the audience and on your message.

THE FIRST 15 SECONDS

- **Establish your space.** If you're speaking from behind a lectern, walk up to it confidently. Place your notes on it. Adjust the microphone. If you're not using a lectern, find your place. Plant your feet.
- **Pause.** Give your audience time to look you over. Take a slow, deep breath. Take another one, paying attention as you do. (Being mindful of your breathing is one of the oldest, most established techniques for making yourself present.)
- **Establish eye contact.** Look one person in the eye for a couple of seconds. Then look at another person somewhere else in the audience. Finally, look a third person in the eye and then—and only then—begin speaking. Make sure you're looking someone in the eye every time you speak.

There may be fifty ways to leave your lover, but there are at least seven ways to start a speech. Try one of these:

- **Tell a personal story.** Stories are easy to follow because they engage our imaginations and emotions. And most people like stories. Avoid the generic "teaching stories" you read on the Internet or in business books—the ones with an obvious moral. Instead, tell a personal story, a humorous or dramatic incident from your life that illustrates the problem you're addressing or the solution you're proposing. When the CEO of a community-based health plan speaks to local groups, she tells the story of her childhood in the poorer section of the city. She reflects on the steps she took to get to where she is today, and she inspires her listeners to make the most of their opportunities.

- **Ask a provocative question.** Don't pose a self-serving question that has an obvious answer, such as "Who would like to make more money?" Ask a question that makes people stop and think. Questions that begin with "what" or "how" are better than ones that can be answered with one word. For example: "How much time do you spend each week in meetings? And how much of that time is well spent?"

- **State a startling fact.** Tell your audience something that will rattle them or pique their interest. To drive your point home, you might want to state two or three facts in a row. For example: "In a recent survey, a thousand business leaders estimated that they spent 70 percent of their average day in meetings. They also stated that a third of those meetings were a total waste of time."

- **Make a bold assertion.** Summarize your thoughts on the matter at hand in one direct statement. (You can always add conditions or explanations later in the speech.) This is no time to be tepid or timid ("Sometimes I think we tend to . . ."). For example: "Meetings are an alternative to work. They're a colossal waste of time, energy, and money and should be banned."

- **Cite a penetrating quote.** Quoting someone is like sharing an opinion (but you can be even more outrageous because someone else said it), and it can give you credibility. For example: "Meetings are indispensable," John Kenneth Galbraith once said, "when you don't want to achieve anything."
- **Refer to a current event.** Bringing up something that has just happened establishes the currency of your topic. Bizarre or humorous incidents work especially well. For example: "On the news yesterday I heard about an executive who refused to go to meetings anymore because . . ."
- **Mix and match.** Combine any number of openings. For example: "How much time do you spend each week in meetings? And how much of that time is well spent? In a recent survey, a thousand business leaders estimated that they spent 70 percent of their average day in meetings. They also stated that a third of those meetings were a total waste of time. Maybe that's why John Kenneth Galbraith said, 'Meetings are indispensable when you don't want to achieve anything.' It's my contention that meetings are an alternative to work and, thus, are a colossal waste of time, energy, and money. They should be banned."

Regardless of why your listeners are there, they have one unspoken hope: that you'll make good use of their time.

Even if you typically speak from a simple outline, I suggest you write out your introduction. Choose any of the opening gambits mentioned.

Start with your second-best material. (Save the best for last.) Memorize your first sentence or two. This is not the time to wing it. (But, of course, the rest of your talk should be conversational, not memorized.) You'll win the audience's attention, respect, and goodwill, plus you'll feel more confident. You'll make the best use of their time . . . and yours.

CHUNK IT

A mason uses bricks, a carpenter uses lumber, and most writers use paragraphs as their basic building blocks. Speakers, though, require a different building material—what I call "chunks."

A cohesive unit of a speech, a chunk consists of two or more of these elements: claims, evidence, illustrations, and audience participation.

1. Claims are assertions—simple declarative sentences—that sum up what you believe to be true and important about a subject. (They also may be called your main point and subpoints, takeaway truths, lessons, and thesis statements.) Your Big Idea is a claim.

The main claim of your speech or presentation may assert that your audience can solve a problem, achieve a goal, or fulfill a dream that is important to them. Examples:

- You can retire a millionaire.
- You can get along with difficult people.
- You can turn warring individuals into a high-functioning team.
- You can outsell all the competition.
- You can become the kind of leader that people admire.
- You can successfully complete your project on time and on budget.

For instance, when Nicholas Negroponte, founder of One Laptop per Child, an organization that aimed to make and distribute inexpensive laptop computers to the world's children, said, "It's an education project, not a laptop project," he was making a claim.

And so was Kathy LeMay, founder and CEO of Raising Change, when she stated, "Our job is to create the space for every person in the world to see the power they have to make a difference."

Your subpoints also are claims. Maybe your listeners don't want—or don't yet know they want—what you're "selling." Or perhaps they don't know how to implement your idea, or are unclear about the concept.

Then your subpoints can provide the answers to these "Why," "How," or "What" questions.

For example, if personal-finance guru Suze Orman were to speak about her book, her main claim would be something like "There are nine steps to financial freedom." Each one of her nine steps would be a subclaim. For example, she might claim (Step No. 2 in her book) "You have to face your fears and create new truths."

2. Evidence is what you cite to explain, support, or prove your claims. It appeals to the intellect. It has to be clear, relevant to your claims, and credible to your audience.

Types of evidence include statistics, survey results, definitions, demonstrations, citations from recognized authorities, charts and graphs, and news reports.

Credibility is the key, but your audience gets to decide what is credible—not you. I once worked with a coalition that was having no success getting the county board of supervisors to declare a health care emergency. That declaration would allow the coalition to begin a program to exchange clean syringes for used ones. (Its aim was to reduce the transmission of bloodborne diseases such as HIV and hepatitis.)

The coalition's strategy hinged on bringing in respected medical researchers and social scientists to counter common misconceptions held by the public. For example, county officials feared that distributing syringes would increase drug usage, and they cited a Canadian study as proof. In response, the coalition flew in that study's lead researcher, who explained that the study—his study—was being misinterpreted and that syringe-distribution programs actually decreased drug usage. In spite of all the experts the coalition produced, the supervisors remained unconvinced.

I pointed out that these elected officials, a proudly conservative lot, didn't care about what researchers thought. They cared about what their constituents thought. They wanted to hear from chambers of commerce, PTAs, churches, and so on. Those were the "experts" the county officials would find credible. Moral: It's not up to *you* to decide who or what is credible; it's up to the *audience*.

3. Illustrations show your claims in action. They don't actually prove anything, but they have the persuasive power of the imagination and emotions working for them. Illustrations are, for most audiences, more convincing than evidence. They're certainly more influential. Leaders should use lots of illustrations, more illustrations, in fact, than evidence.

Types of illustrations include stories, anecdotes, quotes, props, demonstrations, jokes, images, photographs, music, songs, cartoons, magic, flip charts, overhead transparencies, and—used well and in small doses—PowerPoint.

THE SIGNATURE STORY

By far the most powerful form of illustration is the story, and the most powerful form of a story is what professional speakers call a "signature story." It's unique to the storyteller: It's your story, no one else's.

A thoroughly developed signature story will take two to seven minutes to tell and will include a beginning, a middle, and an end; at least one character who undergoes some change; and a satisfying and multilayered application.

In a good signature story you are the main character, which isn't to say that you are its hero. Because of what happens or because of what some other character in the story does or says, you change in some significant way: You change your attitude, outlook, or basic beliefs. You learn an important life lesson.

And it's this new insight that you want to share. If it's a mildly self-deprecating tale from which you emerge humbler but wiser, so much the better.

W Mitchell, a professional speaker, had a remarkable signature story: As a result of two terrible accidents—one on a motorcycle, another in a plane—his face was burned to a crisp, he lost his fingers, and he was paralyzed from the waist down. But with a mantra (and a book) titled *It's Not What Happens to You, It's What You Do About It,* Mitchell concentrated on what he *could* do, not what he couldn't do. In addition to his speaking and writing, he became a radio-TV commentator, a politician, a leading environmentalist, a successful entrepreneur, and, above all, an inspiration to many people with his message of overcoming adversity.

4. Audience participation is, of course, a way of directly involving the audience. It keeps listeners active and engaged. It respects their knowledge, experience, and insight, and it makes them partners with you in creating your speech.

Types of audience participation include Q&A, discussion, group projects, problem solving, audience surveys, dancing, singing, games, magic, movement, and improvisation.

You have to be particularly careful about the way you engage an audience's participation. What energizes one group may alienate another. Imagine, for a moment, trying to get an audience of CPAs involved in a dance.

All the major elements of your speech, traditionally called the *Introduction, Main Points* (3 to 5), and *Conclusion* are really chunks. And it's much easier to construct a speech if you think of creating a bunch of chunks and linking them together.

So, for example, your introduction—Chunk No. 1—could be made up of three or four elements:

Possibility 1. *Illustration* (Start with a story that illustrates the main point of your speech. For instance, "On a recent trip to China, I was repeatedly offered 'genuine' Rolex watches for $5 by street vendors.") *Evidence* (Cite the findings of a survey that supports the main point, such as, say, "A new World Trade Organization study documents soaring international product piracy.") And *Claim* (Conclude the chunk with your main thesis: "U.S. and European manufacturers must unite with governments at home and abroad to stop the sale of knockoff goods.")

Possibility 2. *Evidence* (Cite the findings of a survey that support the main point or your speech—such as the WTO report.) *Illustration* (Tell a story that illustrates the main point—your firsthand observation of Chinese street vendors.) And *Claim* (Conclude the chunk with your main thesis about the need for manufacturers to fight back.)

Possibility 3. *Claim* (Begin with a bold declaration, which is the main thesis of your speech: "Sale of illicitly branded goods threatens to destroy centuries-old, quality manufacturers.") *Illustration* (Tell a story that illustrates the main point: what you observed in China.) And *Evidence* (Cite the findings of a survey that support the main point of your speech: the WTO study's conclusions.)

I illustrate this way of constructing a speech by using different-colored 3-by-5 cards. I label the green cards Claim, the red cards Evidence, the blue cards Illustration, and the white cards Audience Participation. I write examples of each on the back of the cards. Then I simply shuffle the cards. You can create a chunk out of any possible sequence.

Creating a speech using chunks has several advantages:

- **The speech is easier for the audience to grasp.** Each chunk is self-contained. All the chunks work together. If people don't get your message one way, they can get it another way.

- **The speech comes in expected segments.** A chunk is like a mini-speech within a longer speech. It's like a TV show. Viewers are accustomed to watching a program for 7 to 12 minutes before it's interrupted by a commercial. Each chunk is, or should be, no longer than 7 to 12 minutes. (For a 20-minute speech, the opening chunk would be 2 to 4 minutes, each main point would be 5 to 6 minutes, and the conclusion would be 2 to 3 minutes.)
  - **The speech is easier to craft.**
  - **The speech is easier to remember.**
  - **The speech is easy to recycle.** Each chunk can be reused in other forums, because it's freestanding. During a panel session you could, for example, tell a story you previously used in a speech and conclude it with a claim and, voilà, you have a mini-speech or the answer to a question the panel has been asked.

Try working with chunks, and you'll see proof that the whole can be greater than the sum of its parts.

BE—ABOVE ALL ELSE—
A STORYTELLER

Stories are a speaker's—and a leader's—greatest resource. Told properly, they build a bond between the storyteller and the audience and among the audience members themselves. They help audiences see with their imaginations, moving them out of their intellects and into their emotions, which are the wellsprings of action. Tell a good story and you win the audience's attention and willingness to listen.

During one of the gloomiest periods of the Civil War, a delegation of bankers called on Abraham Lincoln. They warned him of the nation's perilous finances, hammering away at the bad news as if he were unaware of it.

"That reminds me of a story," he said, as he often did. Then he told the bankers of a time he boarded with a Presbyterian deacon. "One night I was aroused from my sleep by a rap at my door, and I heard the deacon's voice exclaiming, 'Arise, Abraham, the Day of Judgment has come!' I sprung from my bed and rushed to the window. And there I saw the stars falling in a shower.

"But I looked beyond those falling stars, and far back in the heavens I saw—fixed and immovable—the grand old constellations with which I was so well acquainted. No, gentlemen. The world did not come to an end then, nor will the union now."

Lincoln told stories not just to give his audience hope, as he did in this case, but also to amuse them and to deflate their hostility. To those who criticized him for telling so many stories, he said, "People are more easily influenced and informed through a story than in any other way."

Presidents have always been good at telling stories. (Reagan was a master storyteller.) But business leaders often shy away from telling them, afraid they'll come off as too folksy or "unbusinesslike." And people in technical fields—high-tech, biotech, or the life sciences—think that telling stories is something only "sales reps do." So they end up sounding dry and boring. Nowadays, more and more leaders recognize the value of stories.

Norma Diaz, the newly appointed CEO of Community Health Group (CHG), promoted her organization and its mission—to provide health care to a needy population—by speaking to local groups. She asked for my help because she was dissatisfied with her talks, which she described as informative but a bit dry. She covered all the bases, talking about CHG's history, its member services, its size, and its years of service. "But something's missing," she said.

"What's missing," I told her, "is a story." I asked her to think of some incident that exemplified what was best about CHG. And the floodgates opened. From all the stories she shared, we chose one and built it into her speech. It's about a member, a single mother with limited resources, who called asking for help for her son who was suicidal. He wasn't, however, a member of CHG. The person taking the call could have simply said,

"We're very sorry, but he isn't covered and there's nothing we can do." Instead, he made some calls and put her in touch with other resources. When they talked later, she thanked him for what he did and for giving her and her son hope.

After telling the story, which she related with obvious pride, Norma concluded, "Now, we are a health plan, and we are in the business of offering medical coverage, not hope. But going beyond doing things right to doing the right thing is what we do on a daily basis, and in doing the right thing we give our members hope."

Working that story into her presentation made all the difference. It brought the organization's reason for being to life, and as a bonus it let her natural warmth and passion come through.

More and more corporations and their leaders are telling their stories. Hewlett-Packard, for example, proudly promulgates its founding story, telling how two Stanford graduates began the company in 1939 in a garage in Palo Alto. HP leaders are so proud of their story, in fact, that they have preserved the original garage—California Historic Landmark No. 976—and dubbed it the "birthplace of Silicon Valley." The HP website (www.hp.com/hpinfo/abouthp), for example, goes to extraordinary lengths to chronicle the structure, including photos of the garage, a time line from 1905 to the present, FAQs, news releases, a video, a virtual museum, and feature stories recounting its preservation.

Why do stories hold such magic? For starters, they entertain. And your first duty as a speaker is to capture and hold your audience's attention. Stories also give a sense of structure and meaning to what might otherwise seem like so many disconnected and mind-numbing facts. Further, because they appeal to the little kid in each of us, to our imagination and feelings, stories sidestep our calculating, analytic minds.

What's more, stories are interactive. People let down their guard and lean into a story, causing you to alter your delivery—your words, pacing, volume, and tone. They are *with you* in creating a story.

Listeners grasp your ideas more easily—and retain them longer—if you show them what you mean, not just tell them. They picture the concept more vividly than they would if you just read a bunch of words. Stories appeal to emotions, which is key if you want to move people. Stories linger long after your speech is finished. If the stories illustrate your main points, you've won.

STORY POSSIBILITIES

Here are four kinds of stories leaders can use:

- **Fable.** This is a story crafted to teach a lesson or drive home a moral. It's like a fairly tale for adults. (Fables are often told as if they are "based on a true story," but they have more kinship with urban legends than with actual events.) Stephen Covey, author of *The Seven Habits of Highly Successful People* and leadership guru, tells the fable of a ship's captain who learns of a smaller boat in the distance that refuses to move out of his ship's path. He commands his subordinate to signal ahead and explain that he's the captain of a very large ship and that the other boat *will* move aside. To which the signaler in the distance responds, "This is the lighthouse." He uses the story to introduce what he calls "lighthouse principles," rules that you do not break; you only break yourself against them. The problem with a fable is, it's only good once. If your listeners have already heard it, they tend to stop paying attention or, worse, to stop regarding you as an innovative thinker.

- **Example story.** This type of story—drawn from history, business, movies, or literature—illustrates a point. (You've read several of them already in this book, like the one about George Washington and his spectacles.) On the plus side, they add a sense of independent validation to what you're saying. On the minus side, they are impersonal, since you are in essence talking about someone else's experience. While an example story does reveal something about your character—after all, you chose it—almost anyone else could just as easily tell the same story.

- **Anecdote.** This is a brief incident or scene, told in less than a minute. It's a verbal prop, a metaphor for a concept or process you're explaining. A consultant in customer relations, for example, described her near-traumatic experience at an airport security checkpoint, telling how she had to run in her stocking feet what seemed like two miles to get to her gate seconds before the door was closed. She quoted the gate agent's humorous but welcoming remark as an example of how an employee's thoughtfulness can transform a customer's otherwise negative experience. Anecdotes illustrate and entertain, but they don't fully engage the audience's emotions. So use them freely but don't build your entire speech upon them.

- **Personal story.** A story based on your experience is more fully developed than an anecdote, involving characters and enough action to move from conflict to resolution or insight. It's similar to an example story—but more potent, because it tells the audience something about who you are while imparting a message. The earlier story about the health plan CEO's childhood in a rough neighborhood is such a story.

In a major speech, you should have at least one, and possibly two, personal stories, a few example stories, and as many anecdotes as possible. Be wary of using fables.

What's your story? You need one or, preferably, a number of them. The best ones suit you and your personality. And they embody the message you want to convey.

If you're not accustomed to telling stories and none immediately pops into mind, start by recalling a powerful experience, a turning point that taught you a life lesson. Maybe it was an encounter with someone whose courage, wisdom, or actions forever changed the way you think or feel. Or perhaps it was a simple, everyday event that's emblematic of a broader or deeper truth. Or maybe it was a time when you learned a hard lesson from what seemed like a bitter defeat. Whatever the experience, it made a lasting impression on you, so much so that you want to tell it and will enjoy telling it for years to come.

A writer friend of mine often recounts naïvely entering a cross-country ski race. Hopelessly outclassed and soon struggling alone and dejected through the freezing Minnesota woods, he would have quit a thousand times, except there was no way out. So he skied on, giving up any idea of doing well and instead hoping merely to survive.

As his dreams sank, he remembered a lodge he'd read about in the race brochure. It was about halfway along the route, a place where racers could take off their boots, thaw their frozen feet by a blazing fire, and—he recalls this with stunning clarity—drink a mug of hot spiced cider garnished with cinnamon sticks. That became his new goal. Each time his spirits flagged or his muscles rebelled at doing yet another kick-and-glide, thoughts of the roaring fire and the hot apple cider at the halfway point propelled him on.

He never saw the lodge (perhaps he'd merely *imagined* it), but his fatigue melted into euphoria when he eventually made it to the finish line in an elapsed time not too far from his original goal—and far, *far* better than his worst thoughts.

He uses that story often in speeches to bolster the flagging spirits of other writers:

Perhaps my reeling mind invented the lodge and its comforts as a way of forcing me to trudge on. I don't know. What I do know is that you must keep moving along that snowy path in the woods—even if it's a path paved with blank pages.

No matter how frigid the winds, how achy your limbs, how deep or dark your despair, you've got to persist. Shake off that pessimism by conjuring up your version of that comfy lodge and warming drink.

Maybe you can imagine a bubble bath or a glass of wine waiting at the end of an especially productive day. A nicely turned paragraph or two might be punctuated with a nap in the sun. And a short vacation might mark the completion of the first draft of your novel.

Create such a reward system and persevere, and before you

know it, you'll accomplish more than you dreamed of in your doleful moments. And probably come pretty darn close to your original target.

And next year, who knows? The possibilities are limitless.

You can tell other people's stories, as President Reagan often did. You can tell your organization's story, as the leaders of HP do. Or you can tell your own story, as my friend does. Whichever, you *must* tell stories. Because a speech without a story is flat and lifeless. But a speech *with* a story—the right kind of story, well told—is what leaders give.

A CONFUSED MIND
ALWAYS SAYS NO

If you want your listeners' cooperation—if you want them to say yes to your idea, initiative, project, or pitch—then you've got to be clear about what you want them to do and why they should care.

Clarity won't always win you people's hearts and minds. In fact, there's a chance it may galvanize their resistance. But being *un*clear is sure to make them resist what you want. Confusing people shuts them down. It makes them, at least figuratively, cross their arms in front of their chests, lean away from you, and say *no way.*

So one of the first rules of speaking is: Be clear.

The truth is, any damn fool can complicate something. But it takes skill and effort to clarify a complex subject.

I remember going to an MIT Enterprise Forum that was both a networking opportunity—an hour of mingling over food and drinks—and a showcase for fledgling companies. Attending were a mix of high-tech professionals and those who provide financial services to them.

The president of a start-up was given 30 minutes to talk about his business, its service, business model, and financials, before taking questions from the audience. But after 15 minutes, I walked out. And I wasn't alone. I asked one of others leaving at the same time, "Do you have any idea what that guy was talking about?"

"Not a clue," he replied. "I don't know what his company does. I don't know what its technology does. And as an investment banker, I don't know why I would work with a guy who can't even explain the basics."

If your audiences are often confused ask yourself these questions:

- **Are you yourself confused?** You have to take the time to think through what you're going to say and to identify your goal, main points, and supporting evidence.
- **Are you being overly ambitious?** Trying to accomplish too much in too little time usually results in a confusing mess. Limit yourself to one goal and to one Big Idea per speech.
- **Are you afraid?** Many speakers fear they'll be rejected if they're clear and unambiguous about what they mean and what they want. But leaders would rather stake out a bold position and be rebuffed than hide behind a cloud of misunderstanding.
- **Are you using PowerPoint?** This software allows—even encourages—you to create a succession of slides without tying them together in an organized, logical, or persuasive way. It also abets the tendency to present too much information.
- **Are you trying to be impressive?** Many speakers who come from technical or scientific backgrounds seem to think that being clear is a bad thing; it's a

sign that they aren't smarter than everyone else or don't know more than every-one else. Thus, confusing people becomes almost a badge of distinction: "I must be smart. You couldn't understand a word I said."

"Clarity of mind means clarity of passion, too," the French philosopher Blaise Pascal exclaimed. But how can you make sure you're being clear and not confusing your audience? Here are ten ways:

1. Set one goal. Each speech should have only one goal. (If you want to achieve two goals, give two speeches.) The clearer you are about what you want to achieve, the clearer your speech will be.

2. Start big. Early on, tell your listeners what you're going to tell them. Give them an overview of your talk. Show them the big picture.

3. Limit how much information you provide. People's mental hard drives are pretty full these days. If you give them too much of any type of input—even if they understand and agree with it—they'll stop listening. So give only as much detail as you need to establish or illustrate your main point. Save the rest for another format—say, a white paper, a Web page, or a handout.

4. Make a recommendation. Too many options impede decision-making. Help listeners by presenting two or three of the most compelling choices, along with their pluses and minuses. Then make your recommendation.

5. Keep it conversational. Speak as if you're talking to friends or colleagues. Use simple, plain-English words. Don't try to impress by using big words or jargon.

6. Tell a story. Stories present abstract information or concepts in a simple, concrete fashion that people can picture in their minds. Stories organize a great deal of information in a unified whole and make it memorable.

7. Specify what you're asking of your listeners. Never make people guess what you're after. If you want them to do something, tell them. Then tell them—or better yet, show them—why and how to do it.

8. Keep it bite-size. Present your material in short and simple chunks. Give your audience a little to think about and then stop talking. If they want to know more, they'll ask questions.

9. Don't bore them. Bored people shut down, and shut-down people easily become confused. So vary your tone, volume, and inflection. Vocally emphasize your main points. Don't read your text or your slides to the audience word for word.

10. Go light on the visual aids. When you show people something, they look at it and try to make sense of it. But they stop listening to you in the process. They understand less when they have to look and listen at the same time than they do if they can simply listen or look, one at a time.

ANSWER THESE THREE QUESTIONS

Any speech has to answer three questions: What? How? Why? Depending on the nature and goal of the speech, you'll need to pay more time and attention to one of those questions than to the others.

- **What?** What are you talking about? What's your idea, product, service, initiative, or recommendation? What's the goal you want to achieve? What are the risks and rewards of achieving it? Define whatever it is you're talking about in a way that the audience understands.
- **How?** How did you discover, invent, create, or refine whatever it is you're talking about? How does it work? How will the audience use it? Compare and contrast it with how things are currently done.
- **Why?** Why are you making this proposal or undertaking this project now? Why is this change needed? How will things improve? Why should people care about what you're proposing?

I work with a graphic designer, Len Torres of Primus Design, who handles a lot of complicated assignments from many demanding customers. So he's used to explaining their sophisticated concepts as simply as possible. Over his desk, he's created a poster: "A Confused Mind Always Says No." He says it applies to any type of graphic design.

I think it applies equally well to any type of speech.

SAY IT AGAIN, SAM

You probably know that Ilsa, the Ingrid Bergman character in *Casablanca*, never told the piano player in Rick's Café Américain, "Play it again, Sam." (What she actually said was "Play it once, Sam, for old times' sake." When Sam demurred, she said, "Play it, Sam. Play 'As Time Goes By.' ") But what you may not know is that great speakers often give great speeches because they're giving the same one over and over again.

Take Barack Obama. During the 2008 presidential campaign season, he emerged as one of the most captivating speakers in a field of accomplished, well-coached speakers. Three and four times a day he'd stand before a crowd and, without notes, give a masterful performance. And here's what everyone who followed him knew: He gave the same speech each time, word for word.

Obama, of course, developed new speeches—or, rather, his speechwriters did—from time to time at each new stage of the campaign. He'd tweak each new speech. But once he perfected it, he'd stay with it, shortening it perhaps to suit the schedule or maybe adding a comment or two to lend local color. But for the most part, he delivered *The Speech* the same way each time. No one seemed to mind. In fact, his audiences roared their approval.

He's not alone. Ronald Reagan did much the same thing in his presidential campaign thirty years before. The "I Have a Dream" sequence of Martin Luther King's speech in front of the Lincoln Memorial was lifted verbatim from speeches he'd given at rallies, protests, and church services time and again. And Al Gore's "Inconvenient Truth" presentation is much the same whether delivered in Tokyo or Toledo.

There are three reasons for recycling this way: One, it saves you time, energy, and (sometimes) money. Second, it allows you to give a better speech. And third, it reaffirms your message.

- **Saves time and money**

It takes an investment—of time, money, energy, talent, and knowledge—to create a compelling speech. If you craft your own speech, you must do your research, not just into your topic but also into your audience and the event. Then you've got to select one strong idea, create a clear outline, ruminate about it in your off-hours—including while you're walking or showering or driving. And then you have to come up with stories and quotes and clever ways of saying what you mean. It's hard work.

Even if you hire someone to do most of the writing, you still have to meet with him or her several times. (Because speechwriters don't come cheap, you have to add that expense to the time you invest.) And whether you craft your own speech or pay someone to do it, you still have to practice it. So an important speech can represent many days of your time.

Maybe the event you're speaking at is worth that kind of investment. But the effort makes a lot more sense if, having crafted and practiced a speech, you can give it repeatedly.

My family used to go fishing every summer vacation. We had a running joke about how much each fish cost. We'd total up the expense of fishing—new line, hooks, lures, bait, and license—and divide it by the number of fish we caught. The first fish was always the most expensive. It might cost us $30, a sizable chunk of change in those days. The second fish brought the cost of each fish down to $15. If we caught our limit—usually ten fish a day—each day for two weeks, a single fish was almost free.

You can figure the cost of a speech the same way. Total up your expenses—your time and other people's time at the going rate—and you'll realize how much a speech really costs. If you only give it once, it's a very expensive investment. But if you can give it ten or twenty times, well, that's another story.

- **Produces a better speech**

Very few speeches are so good the first time they're delivered that they can't be improved. Even if you rehearse your speech several times—a necessity but often considered a luxury by most time-pressed leaders—there's nothing like giving it to a live audience. After all, an audience is a speech's cocreator. You can be helped by the way an audience hears what you say, responds to it, and talks about it afterward. Good speakers drop passages that sounded buoyant on paper but fell flat on the stage. They trim sections that prompted yawns, recast phrases that didn't work, and highlight asides that drew unexpected raves.

Also, few performances are good the first time, even with rehearsals. Practicing—whether in front of a mirror (as many speech coaches recommend) or as you're walking about (as I prefer to do)—or performing it in front of a speech coach and a video camera can never match the experience of giving it in front of a real audience. Live performances are the best laboratory. Your listeners give you energy you can't produce on your own. They set your juices pumping. They react in ways you can never predict and, their reactions, will—if you're attentive—improve your delivery.

Professional speakers know this. Most of them develop one speech they give every time they speak. They may perfect a second and a third one with time. But that's it. And when they're working on a new speech, they try it out on safe audiences. Many professional speakers continue to meet with a Toastmasters club so they can have an appreciative audience to try out their new material on.

The first time you give a speech may be good. But it'll get better each time you give it. Say it again and again and again, and it'll get better and better.

- **The message is worth saying again**

Ultimately, there's really only one reason for giving the same speech more than once: What you're saying is worth repeating.

Some leaders act like the proverbial husband who never tells his wife he loves her, because he said it once and she should know. The audience has heard it, they seem to think. That's enough. Don't make me say it again.

Truth is, you can't say the important things too often.

First, because people may not hear you the first time. Even when you're at your best—with a well-honed message delivered at the top of your form—your audience only absorbs a little bit of it. Don't make the mistake of thinking that because you said it, they heard it. (As an experiment, try something I used to do, and still do on occasion when I want to be humbled: When people compliment you on a speech, thank them, and ask them what they heard. You'll be surprised, and not always happily, by what they take away from your speech.)

Second, because your listeners may not think you mean it. People are jaded. They've heard it all before. Been there, done that. And they think, "Yeah, yeah, she is saying that now, but just wait a bit, and she'll be singing a different tune." If you mean something, you have to say it often enough that people take you seriously. "I'm telling you this again, at the risk of sounding repetitious, because it's important and I want to make sure you know it and you know I mean it."

And third, because audiences may forget it. They hear you, they believe you, and still they forget. Not because they want to or because your message is not a priority, but simply because they've got so many other things on their mind. You need to remind them.

Also, remember that your audience is always changing. New people come. Old-timers move on. You can always use this as an excuse: "I know I've said this before. And some of you may be tired of hearing it, but I'm saying it for the sake of the new people in the audience." (It's good for the people who have heard it before to hear it again, anyway.)

Heraclitus, the Greek philosopher, said, "You can't step into the same river twice"—both you and the river are changed the second time around. The same is true for a speech. Even if you give the same speech to the same audience, it's a different speech. You may mean something slightly different by it. And you'll say it in a slightly different way, placing emphasis on different passages, phrases, words. And your audience will take something different from it. In fact, listeners actually *like* hearing the same speech—if it's a good one. We're all akin to little kids who want to hear the same bedtime story over and over.

I used to get asked back year after year to speak to the same group about the same topic. I constantly tried to update my material. Then I noticed that during the Q&A session listeners were asking me to repeat something I'd said before or to tell a story I'd told in previous years. So I went back to giving them the speech they'd already heard and liked before.

Sometimes, of course, you don't want to, or shouldn't, repeat the entire speech. But you can always recycle parts of it. In your annual company-wide speech, for instance, you may have talked about a new initiative the company is undertaking. That section may only have been a third of the speech. But there's no reason you can't lift it word for word and make it into its own freestanding speech.

Reusing your own best stuff is smart. It's not only efficient, it cements your theme with audiences. Or as movie director Alfred Hitchcock proclaimed, "Self-plagiarism is style."

Being Spontaneous Takes Some Planning

Imagine this: You're seated with the other dignitaries, enjoying the fact that, for once, someone else is the featured speaker. But after the speech, which ran shorter than expected, the emcee says, "Our speaker raised some interesting points today. I was wondering what our esteemed guests think." Turning to you, he asks, "Can you say a few words about what you heard?"

Or you've been invited to attend the meeting of a professional association, where you hope to meet prospective clients. But as the meeting gets under way, the association president asks the guests to stand up, introduce themselves, and "say a few words about what you do."

Or you're attending an interdepartmental meeting, sitting in for the director of your department, and the chair turns to you and asks, "Can you say a few words about the projects you all are working on and their status?"

That one short request—*"Can you say a few words?"*—strikes fear in the hearts of leaders everywhere. Call it what you will—ad-libbing, or speaking extemporaneously, spontaneously, impromptu, or off-the-cuff—it means being called upon to give a speech with little, if any, warning. Leaders are never safe. They never know when they might be called on to speak or what they might be asked to talk about.

And yet the most basic, inviolable rule of public speaking is never to speak without being prepared. So you really have only two options: (1) Avoid any gathering where you could even conceivably be asked to speak, or (2) figure out how to prepare for the unexpected.

Speaking spontaneously doesn't mean you can't prepare. It does mean you have to prepare in a different way.

Mark Twain, much admired in his day for his speaking as well as for his writing, observed that "it takes three weeks to prepare a good ad-lib speech." But before you get discouraged, realize that you already have a head start. Think of all the things that you already know and that you've previously spoken about either in conversation, at meetings, or in speeches. You're probably already an expert on lots of topics. First, you know yourself: your experience, interests, values, and job responsibilities. You know your organization: its history, values, mission, and challenges. You know about current events, financial trends, and political issues that affect your business or concern.

And you know about topics that are simply and uniquely of interest to you. That might be fly-fishing in Scotland, Civil War reenactments, or Amish quilts. You know a lot and you have probably talked about all of it in one way or another. All of that—and more—can prepare you for an impromptu speech.

The trick is to take what you already know and to work it into what you're asked to speak about. Sometimes it's easy. If you're asked to say something about your organization or about the main trends affecting your industry or field, that ought to be a slam-dunk. Just breathe a sigh of relief, smile, stand up, and begin speaking.

But sometimes it's not so easy. You may be asked to speak about something you've never thought about. Then you don't have time to think about it. Instead, figure out how to change the subject to something you have already pondered.

Politicians do it all the time. The easiest way to do this is to say, "That's a great question. And it's related to another, more fundamental question." Then pose a question you wish you'd been asked and answer it. If you say something meaningful, it's unlikely anyone will notice that you didn't actually address the question you were asked.

Or you can say, "Here's how I approach this whole issue." That allows you to speak about the big picture, which you know about, without having to address the details or facts, which you may not know about. In either case, be bold. Say your piece and resist any temptation to conclude quasi-apologetically with, "I hope that answers your question."

Different tacks may be needed, depending on how much warning you get, if any. For instance:

If you are attending a meeting. Never attend a meeting without making an effort to see the agenda in advance. Look for items on the agenda titled *updates* or *comments,* and plan how you might speak to them. Even if no agenda item has anything to do with you or your area of responsibility, think of something you might be able to contribute.

If you sense you might be called upon. Maybe you see, for example, the agenda includes time for "comments by guests" and you're a guest. So start organizing your thoughts. You might even have time to write out a few bullet points on scrap paper or a napkin. (That's how the expression "off-the-cuff" came about. People literally used to write crib notes on their shirt cuffs in preparation for a brief speech.)

If you're given no warning. If the request that you speak comes totally out of the blue, it's okay to stall. This is the one situation when you're perfectly entitled to begin a speech by saying polite nothings. Stand up slowly. Establish your space. Take a breath. Look someone in the eye. Smile. Say something like, "I'm delighted you've given me the chance to talk about something that is so important to everyone here in this room." And you might want to add a sentence or two or more. You're not really saying anything at all. You're just giving yourself time to think.

As you're thinking, quickly recall sections of speeches you've already given. If you're asked to comment about industry trends, for example, and you spoke two months ago at your company's annual meeting about "The Challenges Ahead," take one part of that speech—one challenge— and use it. You're not plagiarizing anyone but yourself. Experienced speakers do this all the time.

PLANNED SPONTANEITY

When you're speaking spontaneously, follow these guidelines:

- **Be personal.** Even if you can't pull together the most coherent, insightful, and clever remarks, you can always talk about who you are, what you do, and why you care. Connect with your audience. Be conversational. People may not remember what you said, but they'll remember you and the impression you made.

- **Be opinionated.** This type of speech is like a guest editorial on the op-ed page of a newspaper. Don't give a sweeping survey of everything that's ever been said about the topic. Don't limit yourself to a Joe Friday, "Just the facts" report. Do offer one—and only one—finely focused insight. Make it strong, sharp, and snappy. If you can take a contrarian point of view and say the unexpected, all the better. You want to make people think. And you want them to remember you as someone worth listening to.

- **Be brief.** Brevity is a hallmark of most great speeches. It is the hallmark of all impromptu speeches. Say what you have to say and, having said it, sit down. Thirty seconds to two minutes is enough for most situations. (If the event coordinator or emcee really wanted you to say more, he or she should have asked you in advance.)

"I never resort to a prepared script," said Bishop Fulton Sheen, a popular TV preacher in the fifties and sixties. "Anyone who does not have it in his head to do thirty minutes' extemporaneous talking is not entitled to be heard."

A 30-minute off-the-cuff talk may be a bit ambitious. But surely—with a little preparation—any leader can sound spontaneous for a minute or two.

TAKE A LESSON
FROM KINDERGARTEN:
SHOW-AND-TELL

Kindergartners love recess, naptime, and, especially, show-and-tell. That's where they bring in something from home, show it to their classmates, and tell them about it. They don't stay awake the night before, worrying about what they are going to say. They don't obsess over delivery. And they don't bore their audiences.

So show-and-tell can be a good model for giving a speech.

But don't get too literal about it. Many ways exist to show your audience something. And speeches are especially suited to showing listeners things in their imaginations, using only words and the sound of your voice.

Masterful speakers create images, because they know that long after the audience has forgotten their words, they'll remember the images. Think of Churchill's evocation of the "Iron Curtain" or Herbert Hoover's classic campaign slogan "A chicken in every pot and a car in every garage."

Images in a speech can be created in at least four ways:

1. Use nouns and verbs that conjure up images.

Use concrete, specific nouns and verbs in the active voice—that is, *doing* verbs instead of *being* or *having* verbs.

Consider the beloved 23rd Psalm, which existed in oral form for centuries before being written down. In the King James Version, the psalm is 118 words. And almost every one of those words represents a noun you can see or an active verb. Only two verbs are forms of "to be."

> *The LORD is my shepherd; I shall not want.*
> *He maketh me to lie down in green pastures:*
> *he leadeth me beside the still waters.*
> *He restoreth my soul:*
> *he leadeth me in the paths of righteousness for his name's sake.*
> *Yea, though I walk through the valley of the shadow of death,*
> *I will fear no evil: for thou art with me;*
> *thy rod and thy staff they comfort me.*
> *Thou preparest a table before me in the presence of mine enemies:*
> *thou anointest my head with oil;*
> *my cup runneth over.*
> *Surely goodness and mercy shall follow me all the days of my life:*
> *and I will dwell in the house of the LORD for ever.*

So choose verbs that do something and use them in the active voice. When Lane Kirkland, then-president of the AFL-CIO, spoke in his home state about the benefits the federal government provided, he spoke about his childhood memories. He didn't just say he recalled what it was like to grow up in poverty. Instead, he told listeners, "I remember a South Carolina that was too poor to paint and too proud to whitewash."

And select concrete, specific nouns in place of vague or general ones.

In a commencement address at Knox College, in Illinois, Barack Obama recalled the first press conference he held as a newly elected U.S. senator. He didn't describe himself as just a lowly politician with little standing. Instead he said, "I'm ninety-ninth in seniority, and all the reporters are crammed into the tiny transition office that I have, which is right next to the janitor's closet in the basement of the Dirksen Office Building."

2. Give examples or make comparisons.

Metaphors and similes, used well, are great at communicating images. So complete this sentence, "What I want to describe is like . . ." That's what Reagan—or his speechwriters—did with the Strategic Defense Initiative, the space-based, antimissile system that became known as "Star Wars."

I always ask my clients about their favorite pastimes and urge them to relate some aspect of that activity to whatever it is they're giving speeches about. So, for example, one CEO rides a Harley-Davidson. In one of his speeches, he described a trip he and his buddies took, riding their Harleys through the back roads of the Smoky Mountains. He recalled the coordination and types of communications the trip required. Then he likened that to the type of teamwork and communications his company needed to pull off its next venture.

An executive coach builds houses with Habitat for Humanity. She described the feeling she gets at the end of the project, seeing a family move into its new home. And she compared that feeling to the feeling she wants her listeners to get when they perform a good job well.

A vice president of product development has collected more than 1,000 cookbooks from around the world. In his speeches, he describes the five steps necessary to make a soufflé. Then he walks his audience through five similar steps in using his company's latest product.

The example must be something that listeners can picture in their imaginations. Then link it to what you're talking about, which might be something less visual.

3. Use props.

Props make it easier for the audience to understand—to "see"—what you're getting at. They're memorable. They grab the audience's attention. They communicate information quickly. And they take some of the attention off you, the speaker, which can be a good thing if you tend to get very nervous.

A prop can be any physical object that you interact with onstage. If you use a flip chart à la Ross Perot, it's a prop. If you wave a pair of glasses around to make a point, as Churchill often did, it's a prop. If you stand behind a lectern, even if you don't pound your shoe on it as Khrushchev did when he spoke to the United Nations, it's a prop. (If you do pound the lectern with your shoe, then the shoe is a prop.)

I've seen people use—to good effect—a Frisbee, an alarm clock, scuba gear, a chef's hat and apron, a somersaulting robot, a drum major's baton, a catcher's mask and mitt, a beach ball, and even a bowling ball pulled out of a briefcase.

Props are, almost always, dramatic and entertaining. They can be lighthearted, even silly. But depending on the circumstances, silly may be a good thing. For instance, Tom Antion, a professional speaker, builds one of his speeches around three hats. He dons a baseball cap to describe a company that's young and aggressive. He replaces it with a top hat to talk about a company that has reached a level of maturity. And finally he puts on a safari hat to explain a company's search for new business.

During another speaker's talk, the audience became aware of a cellphone ringing. Finally, the speaker realized it was her phone, and to the audience's dismay she answered it and turned her back on them to talk. As she continued her feigned conversation, the audience grew visibly frustrated. Finally, she said—ostensibly to the person on the other end of the line, but so everyone in the audience could hear—"Don't you hate the way people use cellphones these days? They ignore the people they're with and carry on private conversations that everyone else has to listen to." Then she turned back to the audience, hung up, smiled, and segued into the next part of her speech, which, of course, was about cellphone etiquette.

HOW TO USE A PROP

To use props effectively, follow these rules:

1. Make sure everyone in the audience can see the prop.

2. Focus the audience's attention on the prop before doing something with it.

3. Speak to the audience, not the prop.

4. Show the prop slowly, turning it to face different parts of the audience. Don't let it come between your face and the audience or the microphone.

5. Don't pass your prop into the audience. Always retain control of the prop and of where your audience focuses its attention.

6. Only employ a prop if you're comfortable using it and if it's appropriate for the audience and the occasion.

4. Tell stories.

Stories are like movies in listeners' imaginations. As I've said elsewhere in this book, they're the most powerful element of a speech, and I can't imagine a leader giving a speech without telling at least one story. No need to say more here, because there's an entire chapter devoted to it.

"Vivid images are like a beautiful melody that speaks to you on an emotional level," says TV producer Steven Bochco. "They bypass your logic centers and even your intellect and go to a different part of your brain." And that part of the brain is where your audience can most easily be influenced and inspired. Which is what you want to do, right?

GOING OUT IN STYLE

A speech's conclusion is arguably its most important part. The ending must be brief but powerful, because it's what your audience will remember most.

A strong conclusion—one that sums up the speech, ties it together, and adds an emotional kick—can make even a lackluster speech shine. But an inept conclusion can sabotage the best of ideas.

To get the response you want from an audience at the end of your speech, you need to say something worthwhile. Say it well. And having said it, drive it home.

Remember Howard Beale, the half-crazed newscaster in the movie *Network*? He delivered a 1 1/2-minute rant, which ended with an unforgettable call to action. "I don't have to tell you things are bad," began Beale, who then ticked off a list of things that are bad, anyway. Then he turned up the heat, declaring, "We all know things are bad—worse than bad—they're crazy." In response to the craziness we see all around, he said, we've withdrawn into our houses, into our insulated, isolated little worlds, wanting only to be left alone. "But I won't let you alone."

Then, turning away from his cue cards, he challenged his listeners: "So, I want you to get up now. I want all of you to get up out of your chairs. I want you to get up right now and go to the window, open it, and stick your head out and yell, 'I'm as mad as hell, and I'm not going to take this anymore!!' "

Beale made his case. He roused the audience's emotions. And he ended with an impassioned call to action. *Perfect.*

The conclusion is the most difficult part of a speech to prepare. Perhaps for that reason, many speakers never prepare one. They just stop talking and sit down. The stunned—or relieved—audience claps politely, and class is dismissed.

But the damage has been done. The speaker has undermined whatever power his or her speech contained, and listeners are left vaguely disappointed and unable to figure out what they are supposed to do or feel.

You can do much, *much* better than that by following these dos and don'ts:

DON'T . . .

- **Introduce new material in your conclusion.** Instead, review what you've already said. Summarize your main points. And reinforce the reasons to act.
- **End with Q&A.** Sure, you can take questions at the end of your speech. But once you've answered the last question, don't simply say "Thank you" and be seated. Instead, take another 30 seconds to conclude your speech.
- **Go over your allotted time.** Apologize if you do. Courtesy to your audience, to the meeting planner, to other people who are

on the program, if nothing else, demands that you end on the agreed-upon time.

DO . . .

• **Bring it full circle.** Use an attention-getting technique like the one you used in your introduction. If you opened with a story, finish with a contrasting one. (Also, *stay within the same metaphor.* If your opening story used hunger as a metaphor, for example, your closing story should be something about feeding or being fed.) If you asked a rhetorical question, answer it. If you cited a shocking statistic about a problem, close with a more surprising one about your solution. If you pounded the podium with your shoe, put it back on.

• **Write out your closing and memorize it.** You shouldn't write out and read your whole speech word for word. But it's a good idea to write out the last few sentences and memorize them. They're too important to leave to last-minute improvising.

• **Sound the trumpets.** A great speech moves listeners to action. In as few words as possible, tell your audience what you want them to do. Then inspire them to want to do it. (The best way to so inspire them is to call upon values they cherish and to touch them emotionally.) Carrie Chapman Catt, president of the National American Woman Suffrage Association and tireless supporter of the Nineteenth Amendment to the U.S. Constitution, concluded one of her best-known speeches, "The Crisis," with these words: "Let the bugle sound from the suffrage headquarters of every State. . . . Let the call go forth again and again and yet again. Let it be repeated in every article written, in every speech made, in every conversation held. Let the bugle blow again and yet again. The political emancipation of our sex calls you. Women of America, arise!"

- **Look ahead hopefully.** You needn't be a goody-two-shoes, bright-eyed optimist. In fact, you may feel daunted by the challenge that lies ahead. But you wouldn't be a leader if you lacked confidence in your ability to guide people to something worthwhile. And it's that confidence that you have to communicate, a confidence that looks and sounds a lot like hope. At the end of his first inaugural address, Ronald Reagan told the story of a young solider killed in the First World War and of the message he had left behind. The president concluded, "The crisis we are facing today does not require of us the kind of sacrifice that Martin Treptow [the soldier] and so many thousands of others were called upon to make. It does require, however, our best effort, and our willingness to believe in ourselves, and to believe in our capacity to perform great deeds; to believe that together with God's help we can and will resolve the problems which now confront us. And after all, why shouldn't we believe that? We are Americans."

A bad conclusion—one that ends abruptly, one that never seems to end, or one that simply peters out—can undo almost everything that precedes it.

What specific devices can you use to end a speech powerfully? Here are some examples:

- **A brief story.** Hubert Humphrey once closed a speech with this: "When Franklin Roosevelt died in Warm Springs, Georgia, in April of 1945, he was posing for a portrait and was composing a speech. The President suddenly slumped over. The last words he wrote were: 'The only limit to our realization of tomorrow is our doubts of today.'"

- **A quotation.** Vice President Al Gore concluded his remarks at the Columbine Memorial Service this way: "For now, I know only that my heart weeps with you, and with you I yearn that we may come through this dark passage a stronger and more caring people. For I believe, with all my heart, that 'Earth has no sorrows that Heaven cannot heal.'"

- **A call to action.** This is how Ted Koppel ended his Stanford University commencement address: "Aspire to decency. Practice civility toward one another. Admire and emulate ethical behavior wherever you find it. Apply a rigid standard of morality to your lives; and if, periodically, you fail—as you surely will—adjust your lives, not the standards. There's no mystery here. You know what to do. Now go out and do it!"

Or take Billy Joel's commencement address at the Berklee College of Music: "Have you heard the canned, frozen and processed product being dished up to the world as American popular music today? What an incredible opportunity for a new movement of American composers and musicians to shape what we will be listening to in the years to come. While most people are satisfied with the junk food being sold as music, you have the chance and the responsibility to show us what a real banquet music can be. You have learned the fine art of our native cuisine—blues, jazz, gospel, Broadway, rock and roll and pop. After all this schooling, you should know how to cook! So cook away and give us the good stuff for a change. Please. We need it. We need it very, very much."

• **A wish.** Steve Jobs concluded his commencement address at Stanford by reminiscing about a publication that inspired him: "It was the mid-1970s, and I was your age. On the back cover of the final issue [of *The Whole Earth Catalog*] was a photograph of an early-morning country road, the kind you might find yourself hitchhiking on if you were so adventurous. Beneath it were the words: 'Stay Hungry. Stay Foolish.' It was their farewell message as they signed off. Stay Hungry. Stay Foolish. And I've always wished that for myself. And now, as you graduate to begin anew, I wish that for you. Stay Hungry. Stay Foolish."

• **A rhetorical question.** Ronald Reagan's questions (starting with "Can anyone look at the record of this Administration and say, 'Well done'?"), which were cited above, are one example. From the other end of the political spectrum—Ralph Nader speaking at the NAACP convention—comes another example: "It really is time to ask ourselves, 'How can we allow the rich and powerful not only to rip off people as consumers, but to continue to rip them off as taxpayers?'"

As an old saw has it, "Many speakers need no introduction. What they need are conclusions."

WHY YOU NEED A
SPEECHWRITER—OR
MAYBE YOU DON'T

You're a leader, so in an ideal world, you'd write your own speeches and speak your own mind.

In such a perfect place you'd also have time to read well and widely, be stunningly articulate, and know the intricacies of grammar and syntax. You'd be able to tell a story like a polished raconteur, yet have time for leisurely talks with big-caliber thinkers bursting with insights. Plus, you'd have researchers eager and able to substantiate your conclusions. And best of all, you'd possess the leisure to let your thoughts deepen and mature.

If all that were true, you'd probably also be watching pigs fly.

But because of the scarcity of ideal worlds and winged porkers, you may want to work with someone who'll help create your material. Or *not*, depending on your situation.

In fact, you may already rely on other people to create your written material. Very few leaders these days write what goes out with their names on it—such as letters accompanying annual reports, fundraising appeals, or campaign literature. So if you're using writers to put your thoughts into print, why not let someone write your speeches?

Here's one good reason: Unlike other written pieces, a speech is highly personal. There's always a little distance between who you are and what you write. Memos, letters, opinion pieces, articles, blogs—no matter how personal they are—have a life of their own. They exist in print apart from you. But no such distance separates you from the words you speak. In a speech, words only have life and power because they come out of your mouth, because they ride on your breath and travel on the sound of your voice. Who you are is indistinguishable from the words you speak. So it's always a risky thing to give someone else authority to create those words.

Some people—perhaps you're one of them—shouldn't work with a speechwriter. They're just naturally great speakers who know what they're talking about and, with little advance notice, can deliver a polished, near-perfect speech. Some work best just from an outline, ad-libbing as the spirit and the audience move them. And some speakers are so opposed to letting anyone put words in their mouth that they can't even imagine working with a speechwriter.

Plus, some situations militate against working with a speechwriter. For starters, speechwriters can be expensive. If you're not prepared—or able—to shell out a tidy little sum, don't bother looking for someone. And if you're under a really tight deadline, you simply may not have the time to find the right person and bring him or her up to speed.

The first rule of working with a speechwriter—if doing so makes sense for you—is to find someone who will capture *your* thoughts and put them in *your* words. People often hope that a speechwriter will make them sound like someone else—like Churchill or FDR or Margaret Thatcher—like anyone but themselves. But what you *really* want is someone who will make you sound like you at your best. A good speechwriter will use your words and speech patterns. He or she will clean them up and polish them, of course, but the end result will still sound like you.

The second rule is to invest time in working with a speechwriter. If you delegate the entire responsibility for creating your speech to the professional, you won't be happy with the final product. The more you make yourself available to the speechwriter, the more you share your insights and thinking process, and the more you talk with him or her, the better job the speechwriter will be able to do.

HOW TO INTERVIEW A SPEECHWRITER

In the real world, where time is at a premium and audiences have become more discriminating, a speechwriter might be able to help you. But understand, finding one is not as easy as it sounds, because you're really looking for a partner. You're the content expert; the writer is the communication expert. You need someone who knows the trade and who's compatible with you.

Here are some questions you might ask.

- **Experience.** How long have you been writing speeches? With whom have you worked? What type of client do you work with best? (You don't want to be the one breaking in the speechwriter. Also, beware of a person who blithely tosses about the names of clients. You want someone who will respect your confidentiality.)

- **Area of expertise.** Do you mostly write speeches or do you also write press releases, brochures, information kits, websites, and the like? (Call me biased, but I believe the more types of writing a person does, the less suited he or she is to writing speeches.)

- **Work samples.** Can I see some examples of your work? (Because a speech is the client's property—not the speechwriter's—you may not be able to see the whole range of his or her output.)
- **Familiarity with the issues.** What do you know about my field or industry? What do you know about the issues I'll be addressing? (You can't expect the speechwriter to know as much as you do. But you want someone who is well read and a quick study.)
- **The process.** How often will we meet? What will happen at those meetings? Will we meet face-to-face or by phone? How much of my time and energy should I plan on investing? (This has got to mesh with your schedule.)
- **Benefits.** Why should I use you? What are you going to do for me that I couldn't do by writing the speech myself?
- **Price.** How much is this going to cost? At what points in the process will the payments need to be made?

Years ago I got hired to write a speech for a university president. He was set to speak for 20 minutes at the graduation ceremony, marking an important anniversary of the school. It was a rush job, and the president was so busy he kept rescheduling our appointments. His assistant ended up acting as an intermediary, conveying his short and cryptic comments to me. He had only the vaguest idea of what he wanted to say—maybe something about the role of the university in contemporary society, maybe something about how education has changed over the years, maybe something about the need for graduates to become citizens of the world.

In spite of my many attempts, I never once spoke with him, either face-to-face or by phone. The speech I produced was general, generic, and—to me, at least—an embarrassment. And, of course, I learned what a string of recent presidential speechwriters have learned: Those with frequent and open contact with their clients can create great speeches; those who don't, can't.

At the very least, you should expect to meet with a speechwriter—in person or by phone—four times.

During your first meeting, the speechwriter will want to discuss the basics: the event, the audience, your goals, your central idea, and two or three main points.

In the second meeting the two of you will review the purpose of your speech and its main points. The speechwriter will propose a detailed outline and discuss supporting material he or she has identified, asking for your input and go-ahead.

By the third meeting you should have a rough draft of the speech. Read it through silently the first time to make sure it makes sense. If you don't understand anything, underline it. It will need to be revised. Then read it through aloud. Underline any word or phrase that gives you trouble. Those words will need to be revised. Ask yourself: Does it capture what I know to be true and what I want to say?

The fourth and last meeting is, or should be, for minor adjustments and tweaks.

In emergencies, of course, you can condense this process. It's possible to write a speech the day before it's to be given—most speechwriters have the psychic scars to prove it. But that's not preferable. Instead, depending on your availability and on the speech itself, allow from one month to four months.

Working with a good speechwriter will give you a speech you'll be proud of. But just as important, it'll teach you the process of creating a great speech so that someday, maybe, you'll be able to do it by yourself.

PART FOUR

A Masterful Delivery

DELIVER THE REAL YOU

The executive director of an advocacy group asked for help on a 30-second radio spot. A PR person who'd written the script was in the recording studio acting as the director. The climax of this short piece was "I'm outraged. And you should be, too."

Though bright, articulate, and dedicated, the executive director didn't sound outraged. His "I'm outraged" sounded more like "I'm concerned" or "This bothers me—a bit." Before I could say anything, the PR person jumped in. "You don't sound outraged," she said. Then, quite convincingly, she demonstrated how to sound outraged.

Six more takes did not dramatically change my client's delivery, which remained flat and passionless. Finally, with both of them looking frustrated, the PR person turned to me and pleaded, "Can't you do *something* with him?"

I pulled him aside and asked, "On a scale of one to ten, how outraged are you about this issue?" He didn't understand, so I said, "Of all the issues we face today, this one doesn't bother me very much. I'd give it a one or two on my outrage scale. What about you?" He smiled sheepishly and agreed.

We talked a little more, and then I suggested he change his script to "I think it's wrong. And we should do something about it."

And that worked, because he could say it with conviction and with an appropriate, even if subdued, level of passion. The way you deliver a speech can never be separated from who you are—how you naturally present yourself—from the message you want to communicate, and from the nature of the event itself.

Most speech coaches I come across are little more than stage directors. They tell speakers how to stand and move and what kind of gestures to use. They're always urging their clients to use more vocal variety. And like that PR person, they try unconsciously to refashion their clients into clones of themselves.

But delivery involves using *your* body and *your* voice to communicate *your* message. It's more than technique. It's about projecting your authentic self as powerfully as possible. The verb *to deliver* originally meant "to set free or to release." I don't know what's being freed—who you are or the message you want to communicate. Perhaps a little of both.

To improve your delivery without sounding—or feeling—like you're giving a stage performance, try doing these things:

- **Be yourself.** It takes hard work, practice, and a great deal of self-confidence to be yourself in front of an audience. Much of what you have to do is *unlearn* a lot of what you've been taught about giving a speech. Stop imitating anyone else, even speakers you admire.

  Bob Newhart, the comedian known for his deadpan delivery and for playing the "straight man" surrounded by bizarre cast members and even more bizarre events, told an interviewer about one of his most frustrating professional experiences. A guest director for the long-running *Bob Newhart Show* kept pressing him to speed up his delivery and to show a bit more emotion. Finally, in exasperation he said, "Look, I *do* Bob Newhart. That's what I do. That's all I do."

Learn from others and how they look and sound in front of an audience. Study leaders whose speaking you admire. Maybe even work with a coach. But never *do* anyone other than yourself.

- **Be bigger and louder.** I know I just urged you to be yourself. Now I'm adding a qualifier: Be yourself, only *bigger* and *louder*. The stage is no place for shrinking violets who shy away from the spotlight. Nor is it the place for quiet, understated, and undersized performances.

When I'm rehearsing speakers, I usually ask them to talk through their speech with me, one on one, as we sit around a table or across the desk from each other. They're usually clear and animated. They use a natural range of gestures, and they have a fair amount of vocal variety.

I say, "That was great. Now stand up there on the stage and say it exactly the same way." Nine times out of ten, they change before my eyes as they walk up to the stage. They shrink. And they become stilted. The life drains out of their voice and they keep their arms locked by their sides or they clasp their hands in a gesture I've never seen them use before. They go into what I call their "speaker's mode."

My task is to get them to speak the same way they did when

they were simply talking to me, but to add a bit more life—to be bigger and louder.

When you're in front of an audience, use the same gestures you normally do, only exaggerate them. And speak louder. It's amazing how increasing your volume almost always increases your voice's liveliness and power.

• **Be passionate.** Don't speak about something you don't care about. And if you care about it, show it and make it personal. Don't act as if you're simply laying out a reasonable proposal, coolly analyzing the merits of both sides before rationally arriving at a conclusion. (At times, of course, such as when making a highly technical presentation, that may be exactly what you need to do.) Instead, throw yourself into your speech. I'm not asking you to feel something you don't or to act out a feeling you don't have. I'm asking, instead, that you let how you really feel show.

I worked with a man, for example, who was the lead presenter on an oral proposal for a defense contract to provide virtual training for soldiers preparing to serve in Iraq. He was a retired colonel in the armored divisions, a dedicated, no-nonsense, straight shooter who spoke with quiet intensity. During rehearsals he gave a well-organized, well-reasoned talk outlining the strengths of his company's proposal. But he sounded as if he were following a rule book on how to give a persuasive presentation. He was good, but he sounded impersonal and detached, and I knew from having worked with him on developing the proposal that he was anything but impersonal and detached.

"I know you want to win this contract for your company," I said. "What I don't know, or what I can't hear from listening to your presentation, is *why* you want to win this contract. Why do you care?"

Reaching into his briefcase, he pulled out a letter from a field commander in Iraq. He read the letter to me and, when he got to a line that said, "Your program saves lives. I know, because it saved mine," he choked up. Then he said with total conviction, "That's why I'm supporting this proposal. Because I know what we do saves the lives of warfighters like the ones I used to lead in battle."

I asked him not to change a word of what he had already planned on saying, but to change the way he said it. "I want you to say it, knowing what you know, feeling what you feel." He told me after his team had won the contract that making that one small change affected everything he said or, at least, how he said it.

Most speakers keep a little distance between who they are and what they say. It's as if they're telling the audience, in effect, you can take or leave what I say, just don't reject me. But real leaders don't want to distance themselves from their message. They let their passion show.

- **Be dramatic.** A little drama gets people's attention. Yet most leaders are so worried about presenting a powerful image that they end up looking wooden. They're afraid they won't be taken seriously or given the respect they think they're due if they pump up their delivery and get passionate or playful. Yes, you have to be yourself onstage—but you also have to be bigger, louder, and, indeed, more dramatic onstage than you are off.

Tell a story, and when you do, throw yourself into it, using pauses and voices and maybe even sound effects. (A good way to practice is to read a story aloud to a child when no adults are around.) Use a prop. Raise your voice. Or whisper (into the microphone, of course). Pause, not to think of what you're going to say, but to add emphasis (i.e., drama) to what you just said.

Most of us are inhibited speaking in front of a crowd. We tend to shrink—to limit our enthusiasm, the range of our voice, and the size of our gestures—when we should be doing exactly the opposite.

A speech coach I worked with early on helped me break through my self-imposed restraints. He kept urging me to be bigger, louder, more expressive. And I kept resisting him. Finally he asked, "What are you afraid of, besides making a fool of yourself?"

"Well, besides that," I said, "I'm afraid I'll be too theatrical." He asked what that would be like, and I said, "I don't want to sound like Laurence Olivier."

"Show me," he replied. I looked perplexed, so he said again, "Show me you can be too theatrical. I love Laurence Olivier. Show me you can sound like him."

Of course, I couldn't even come close. That coach taught me a lesson I impart to my clients. We clamp down on our expressiveness, fearing we'll go too far, be too dramatic, when in truth most of us couldn't do it even if we tried.

Few people—in my experience, fewer than 1 out of 100—have to worry about going over the top. Most of us stay way too far under the radar.

WOULD YOU RATHER BE IN THE CASKET OR GIVING THE EULOGY?

Jerry Seinfeld does a bit where he points to surveys showing that people's number one fear is public speaking, while their second-worst dread is death. "Does that seem right?" he asks. "To the average person that means that if they have to go to a funeral, they'd be better off in the casket than giving the eulogy."

That was almost literally the case in one situation I witnessed. The CEO of a start-up life-sciences firm was slated to give a 20-minute pitch four times on the same day to different groups of venture capitalists, each followed by 10 minutes of Q&A. It was a great opportunity even to be chosen to address these money moguls. And it was, apparently, an even greater cause of anxiety, because before he had the chance to give his first talk he had a heart attack and collapsed. He survived, but the experience taught me to take people seriously when they say they'd rather die than give a speech.

When it comes to public speaking, there are actually two types of fear. There's the kind that people usually think of. Let's call it stage fright. It can produce physical symptoms—sweating, trembling hands, shaky knees, a racing heartbeat, difficulty breathing—as well as memory lapses and problems verbalizing. These reactions can range from mild to extreme, from irksome to incapacitating.

Can you—*should* you?—eliminate stage fright? That wasn't possible for Lincoln, Churchill, Adlai Stevenson, or many other famous orators. And it may not be possible for you. One of my clients, a wildly successful neurosurgeon and an outwardly confident speaker, confessed he couldn't sleep the night before he was scheduled to lead a silent prayer. But techniques and strategies exist for dealing with this type of fear, ways experienced speakers use to turn it into energy to boost their performance. (I'll get to those shortly.)

But there's another type of fear that rarely gets acknowledged. It's the fear that wells up whenever we lay bare our authentic self. It's a formidable challenge to go in front of others and take a stand, giving voice to the truths we've learned the hard way, not knowing if we—not just our ideas, but we, *ourselves*—will be accepted or rejected. No techniques or strategies are known to quell this unnamed fear. The only remedy is courage.

You can diminish stage fright and turn it to your advantage, but I don't think you can ever get rid of this other type of fear, and I don't think you should try. When you speak like a leader, no matter how accomplished and experienced you may be, you should always feel at least a tinge of fear. It's a sign you're being real. It's proof that even when others play it safe by saying what everyone else is saying, you dare to say—flat out and unequivocally—what you mean.

That being said, what can you do about that first fear, stage fright?

When you perceive a threat—and an audience can appear mighty threatening—your body instantaneously reacts. It shifts into a fight-or-flight mode, flooding your system with adrenaline. Your pulse rate increases. Your breathing speeds up and gets shallower. You start sweating. Blood rushes oxygen to the large muscles of your body—your arms and legs—preparing them for action, while the higher region of the brain, the one that governs memory and verbal ability gets less oxygen. If you don't attack something or run away—if you just stand there, gripping the lectern—the unspent adrenaline will cause your arms and legs to shake.

Stage fright can make your movements stiff and unnatural. It can slow your thinking process to a standstill. It can make you unable to remember specific phrases, words, facts, and figures. If you're a man, your voice may flatten out and become monotonous. If you're a woman, your voice may rise in pitch and become artificially animated. It isn't pretty. But if you carve your stage fright down to a manageable size, your natural style, true personality, wit and humor, and, indeed, message will come through strong and clear.

To take control of your symptoms of fear:

- **Be prepared.** If you stand before an audience without having planned what you want to say, you *should* be nervous. It's your body's way of saying, "You fool. Don't do this to me again." Dale Carnegie, the first guru of American public speaking, wrote, "Only the prepared speaker deserves to be confident."
- **Breathe.** Remember: Fear makes you breathe fast and shallowly, almost like you're panting or—worse—hyperventilating. Counteract this by taking several slow, deep breaths whenever you feel nervous and especially in the minute or two before you

begin speaking. This type of breathing, sometimes called belly breathing or abdominal breathing, is one of the oldest and most common techniques of meditation. Practiced correctly, it will calm your nerves faster than anything else.

• **Practice in front of safe audiences.** Seek opportunities to speak where there's little at stake. Consider joining a Toastmasters club. (You can find a club near you at www.toastmasters.org.) Toastmasters clubs have weekly meetings, a structured process that will ease you one baby step at a time into speaking, and a very supportive atmosphere.

• **Befriend the audience.** Work the room before your presentation begins. Introduce yourself and shake hands. Get to know at least a few people so those you're speaking to aren't simply a nameless crowd. While you're speaking, seek out friendly faces. Imagine you're having a conversation with them, one person at a time, rather than giving a speech. Have their best interests at heart. And remind yourself that you're speaking not to foist something unwanted on them but to share something that will benefit them in some way.

• **Avoid caffeine or alcohol** in the hours before your talk. You don't need any more stimulants.

• **Don't call attention to your nervousness.** Don't tell people you're nervous. If your hands are shaky, it's okay to rest them on the sides of the lectern, but avoid gripping it with what will look and feel like a death clasp. Avoid picking up your notes or the water glass or anything else that will accentuate the shaking.

- **Put on your game face.** Know that you don't look as nervous as you feel. You judge yourself by how you feel inside—your racing heart, your sweaty palms, your churning stomach—but people judge you by what they see on the outside. And you never, or almost never, look as nervous as you feel. Let people continue to think that you're confident, and after a while you'll begin to feel confident.

WHEN DO YOU GET NERVOUS?

Different people get nervous at different times. The trick is to recognize your fear as soon as it occurs, so you can address it before it grows out of proportion. Here are the most common times that people get anxious and some strategies for dealing with it:

- **Always.** Some people have such an unrelenting fear of speaking that they're always on guard, vigilantly steering clear of any situation where they could possibly be expected to give a speech. They may adamantly refuse to give a project update, for example, even though they are the project leader and their refusal will cast them in a negative light. Or they may turn down a promotion, fearing that the new position will require them to make presentations. This type of fear has no easy antidote. You can begin to address it by acknowledging how much your fear is holding you back, damaging your career, or keeping you from having the impact you'd like. If even the thought of joining a Toastmasters club is too intimidating, you may want to seek out a speech coach.

- **The week before.** Some people begin feeling anxious seven to ten days before the big event, about the time they realize they can't put off preparing for it any longer. The very thought of doing something overwhelms them. (It's a vicious circle. Fear of failure keeps them from preparing. Speaking without being prepared ensures failure. Failure makes them afraid.) Try this instead: Acknowledge your fear, and do one small thing. Break your preparation into manageable pieces—for instance, analyzing your audience, doing some basic research, determining your goal, outlining your talk—and start by doing just one.

- **Immediately before.** The majority of people report that they get most nervous in the minute or two right before speaking. As they're being introduced or as they wait for the meeting to begin, they feel a sudden spike in nervousness. It continues through the first 30 to 60 seconds of their speaking, gradually tapering off as they continue. This is when you need to take your slow, deep breaths. Be conscious of your breathing. And remind yourself that the audience wants you to succeed and that you have your listeners' best interests at heart.

- **Afterward.** A few people get nervous after it's all over. They replay the speech in their minds, fixating on everything they did wrong, berating themselves for their poor performance, and shrugging off every compliment they received. They work themselves into a high state of anxiety. What's needed here is an attitude adjustment. Be kind to yourself. No one improves by having a harsh critic—even a harsh inner critic—hovering over them, pointing out their mistakes, and belittling them. Settle for progress instead of perfection. Make it your aim to give a "good enough" speech, not a flawless one.

When you think about it, isn't it somewhat silly to be more afraid of giving a speech than of anything else? I suspect that if that oft-quoted survey had been worded differently, the results would have been different. Imagine being asked, for example, what would scare you more: Giving a speech or losing someone you love? Giving a speech or being diagnosed with a painful, incurable disease? Giving a speech or getting fired? If you answered, "giving a speech" to any of the above questions, you seriously need to reexamine your priorities. A lot of events deserve infinitely more apprehension.

It's okay to be afraid of giving a speech. You're in good company. But please keep your fear in perspective. And when it does get to be too much, do something about it. Take the words of Eleanor Roosevelt to heart: "I believe that anyone can conquer fear by doing the things he fears to do, provided he keeps doing them until he gets a record of successful experience behind him."

HAVE I REACHED THE PARTY
TO WHOM I AM SPEAKING?

Ernestine, the sarcastic and imperious telephone operator played by Lily Tomlin on the old *Laugh-In* show, used to ask in her pinched, nasal voice, "Have I reached the party to whom I am speaking?"

It was a ridiculous question. (That's why it was funny.) Of course, she'd reached the party to whom she's speaking. Whom else could she be speaking to?

But for a public speaker, it's not such a ridiculous question. In fact, it might be the quintessential question. Because a speech isn't just about what words are said, or for that matter, what words are heard.

A speech is about whether the speaker truly reaches—*makes a connection with*—the audience. If there's no connection, there's no speech.

Years ago, my best-ever speech teacher, Fred Baumer, kept trying different methods to help me overcome what other people called my aloofness or my reserve. Fred realized I was working so hard internally to keep my panic at bay that I had no energy to reach outside myself to the audience. Nothing we tried worked.

Finally, he asked me who my favorite comedian was. I told him Johnny Carson. Fred then asked me what I liked about Johnny. I said he had some great material, but what I really liked was how he played off the audience's reaction when one of his jokes bombed. He'd tell a joke. No one would laugh. In fact, some would moan.

That's when Johnny came alive. He'd ad-lib some funny retort or he'd look ridiculously pained and then use the audience's disapproval as a springboard to some other funny story. And he'd end up getting more laughs than if the audience had liked the original joke. Comedy, at least for Johnny Carson, wasn't about telling jokes and making the audience laugh. It was about playing off the audience or, better yet, playing *with* the audience.

The same is true for a great speech. It's not merely about speaking words—even well-chosen words—and making the audience think. A great speech is about what happens between the speaker and the audience.

In other words, you reach the audience by speaking not *to* them, but *with* them. Take Ronald Reagan, Bill Clinton, and Tony Blair. In spite of vastly different political beliefs, all three had an ability to reach out and touch their audiences. You may not remember exactly what they said, but you probably recall the extraordinary effect each had on his listeners.

Reaching the audience to whom you are speaking is sometimes called building rapport, but it's really something more sophisticated. It's not something you can do on your own. It's something that takes place between you and the audience.

Reaching the audience involves attention, respect, and affection. More important, it involves *mutual* attention, respect, and affection.

• **Attention.** You should give and expect attention. You give the audience your attention by learning as much as you can about them before speaking, by tailoring your message to them and to their needs and concerns, by interacting with them before taking the stage, and by doing whatever you can onstage to bridge the divide between them and you.

And you demand their attention. Yes, you must make the first move to reach out to your audience. But what's often overlooked is that you have the right to expect them to reach back. It's not entirely up to you.

If you think or act as if making a connection with the audience is entirely your responsibility, you're setting yourself up for failure. First, you'll make yourself work too hard. And second, you'll let the audience off the hook. You have the right to demand the audience make some investment. If you have to do all the work from the beginning, it will never get easier.

The most effective technique for asking for an audience's attention is silence. Take the stage. Arrange your notes (if you have any) and adjust the microphone. Look at your audience. And don't say anything. Pause. Wait longer than you think is necessary, right, or proper. (Being silent in front of an audience takes moxie.) The audience will quickly settle down and turn to you. Then, and only then, speak.

James Humes, a speechwriter for five American presidents, wrote, "Every second you wait will strengthen the impact of your opening words. . . . Stand, stare, and command your audience, and they will bend their ears to listen."

• **Respect.** Of course, you want the audience's respect. Without it, there's little you can accomplish as a leader. And as much as possible, you want to gain that respect before you begin speaking. You do that partly by your reputation, by what the audience already knows and feels about you. You do that partly by what the audience learns about you from the formal introduction that someone else makes. And you do that partly by how you handle yourself in front of the audience. Your appearance—how you dress, stand, and move—and the pitch, timbre, and volume of your voice go a long way toward winning or losing your audience's respect. The more respectful you are of them, of their time and values and interests, the more respect they will give you.

That raises a question: Must you respect an audience in order to speak to them? I'd say, yes, you do. You don't have to respect their opinions, actions, or attitudes. You might disagree with them and even find their beliefs and behaviors objectionable. But if you don't respect them as people, you shouldn't talk to them. Leaders often go into groups whose opinions or agendas they oppose and speak to them, sometimes heatedly, in order to change them.

• **Affection.** By affection I mean liking. You want, if possible, for the audience to like you. That doesn't mean they'll love you, feel warm and romantic feelings toward you, or want to take you home to meet the family. It does mean they enjoy being in your presence. The easiest way to do this, of course, is to be likable. The next best way to do this is to let the audience know how similar you are to them. (One of the rules of influence is this: We tend to like people who are like us.)

That's why Robert Gates, speaking at Sophia University in Tokyo, began his speech "As a historian and former university president, I am particularly gratified to be here with you in this center of learning." He didn't announce—although the audience clearly knew—that he was also the U.S. Secretary of Defense.

So you want them to like you. But must you like *them*? It helps immeasurably if you do, but it's not required. If you actively dislike them, however, you'd be much better off not speaking to them. They will sense your antipathy and will reciprocate. At the very least, even if you don't enjoy being with them, you must care about them in the sense that you want them to have what's in their best interest.

HOW TO CONNECT

To connect with your audience, try these techniques:

- **Know your audience.** You wouldn't talk about a subject you don't know, would you? So don't talk to an audience you don't know. The more you learn about them, the better you'll be prepared. At the very least, find out how many people are expected to attend your talk, what they already know about your subject, and how they feel about it.

- **Work the room.** Arrive early. Check out the physical arrangements—the room setup, the microphone, the computer, and projector (if you really have to use one). And then talk to people as they arrive. Get to know some of them personally. It will make you more confident. And it will begin the process of building a connection.

- **Address their concerns.** Don't talk about your expertise. Use your expertise—what you know about your subject—to show your audience how they can solve a problem or achieve a goal that's important to them. Talk about what they care about, and they'll care about what you say.
- **Look them in the eye.** Eye contact, in Western cultures at least, establishes credibility. Look one person in the eye at a time. Speak to that person for 5 to 7 seconds. Then establish eye contact with someone else in another part of the room.
- **Offer a conversation, not a speech.** The very thought of giving a speech makes most people break out in a sweat, and it makes them look and sound unnatural as they're speaking. Think instead of holding a conversation with your audience. Speak the way you normally do, only with more preparation and attention. Use personal pronouns (I, you, and we) and contractions (I'm, you're, and we'll).

When you make an effort to make a connection, you'll be on your way to building a relationship and establishing trust. Do that, and the audience will be much more likely to give you their attention and cooperation. Thus, like the Lily Tomlin character, you'll actually be reaching the party to whom you are speaking.

WRITING, READING, AND TALKING

Today's audiences want speeches that sound conversational. But listen to the conversations around you. They ramble, stumble, stutter, and stop. They often change direction in midstream, then trail off and fail to finish a thought. And they're full of meaningless words and vocal hiccups like *um, er, ah*, and *ya know*.

So really what you want is to mirror not ordinary conversation but the kind of dialogue that's spoken by smart, thoughtful, articulate, and witty people in plays and movies. In short, you want your speech to sound like a *scripted* conversation.

You should rarely read a speech word for word. But you can strengthen just about any speech by writing it out.

While you may not have the time or inclination to write out all your speeches, *always* write out these three types of speeches:

- **The policy speech.** This is a onetime speech that announces a major new development, direction, merger, acquisition, or other policy change. If it's likely to be quoted or cited in the media, write it out.

- **The stump speech.** You need at least one stump speech (and as many as three) that you'll give over and over again to different audiences. Politicians do this all the time as they barnstorm their state or the nation, localizing their overall theme. The idea is to write one good speech, then tweak it a little for each new audience. For instance, if you're visiting different offices or branches of your company, come up with a central message for all employees, then customize it a bit for that specific group. Or if you regularly speak to professional associations or civic groups in order to promote your business or to advance your agenda, create one speech that you can use over and over again.

- **The watershed speech.** This is a talk you'll give just once, but that has a lot riding on it. You need to shine because you're addressing, say, all your peers at the national convention. Or you're speaking to policymakers or other leaders who are expecting you to blaze a new trail.

Now, you'd think that the more you know about a subject, the less likely it would be that you'd need to bother writing out a speech. But actually the reverse is true: The more knowledgeable you are, the more you need to pin it down. That's because you know so much that you have to get rid of clutter, all that interesting stuff that's in your head but isn't vital to your listeners.

"When a person's knowledge is not in order," wrote nineteenth-century philosopher and social scientist Herbert Spencer, "the greater will be the confusion of thought." Writing out your speech helps reduce that "confusion of thought."

It takes skill to present a Big Idea clearly and persuasively—and still keep the speech conversational. That's where writing out a speech pays big benefits, such as helping to:

- **Clarify your thinking.** Writing out your remarks forces you to be clear, logical, and precise. Often, it's the details—not the generalities—that make or break your case. And writing forces you to deal with details and how they fit (or don't fit) together.
- **Sharpen the focus.** Most of your speeches are—or should be—short and pointed. The paradoxical thing is, shorter speeches require more effort. You can't afford to ramble, get off topic, or address too many issues. If you talk for 5 minutes, you'll say roughly 600 to 750 words. That's not a lot. So you'll need to get right to the heart of the matter. Writing forces you to do that.
- **Tighten the connections between the parts.** The weakest parts of most speeches, at least structurally, are the transitions. If you simply write out a list of bullet points or of talking points, you'll assume that there's a clear and logical bridge from one point to the next. But that bridge may not be as clear as you think, or it may be clear only in your mind, because you've given it considerable thought. Writing out the speech will force you to be explicit about how to get from one point to the next.
- **Serve as a rehearsal.** Writing out your speech makes sure you know what you're talking about. You have to think through your main points, the logic, the supporting evidence,

the possible objections. You have to eliminate distractions, digressions, and filler. And having done all that, you're ready to go on.

- **Provide security.** When you have a written text either before you or nearby, you never have to worry about choking. You can look your script over right before going on and in the worst-case scenario, you can always refer to it.

So if writing out a speech brings big benefits, how exactly do you go about it?

Well, of course, before putting pen to paper (or cursor to screen), you must do your research. Find out as much as possible about the event, the audience, and your topic. More specifically, know your goal: What do you want to accomplish? What do you want the audience to know, feel, or do as a result of hearing you speak?

Then develop your one Big Idea. What is it? Is it substantial enough to build a speech around? Does it have the power to (positively) change your listeners' lives?

Next, create an outline. Don't bother with the Roman-numeral kind of outlining you may have learned in high school. Simply start with your main points. (Three are best.) Add an introduction and a conclusion. Then add some bullet points under each main point, answering one of the following questions: *What? How? Why?*

Then write out the speech word for word. You don't have to start at the beginning and work your way through it. Many people develop the body of the speech first—those three main points—and then go back and write out the introduction. Finally, they write out the conclusion. As you write, read it aloud. Remember, you're writing for the ear, not for the eye.

WRITING A SCRIPT

When you're writing a script, learn from radio and TV announcers who use a format that allows them to avoid sounding like they're reading. Even if you aren't planning to read the script word for word, using this style will help you in two ways.

First, it'll teach you how to write for your audience's ears, not for their eyes. And second, it'll make it easier for you to remember as you read it over and over in rehearsal.

Try this:

- **Set up your page for maximum readability.** Use a serif typeface (such as Times New Roman, Garamond, or Palatino) at font size 16 or18. Do not use all capitals. (Save ALL CAPS for words you want to emphasize.) Set the line spacing at 1.5 or 2. Set the right and left margins at half an inch and the tab stops at every quarter inch.
- **Number each page in large print.** Pages have a perverse habit of getting out of order, and you don't want to shuffle through your script in front of an audience searching for your place.
- **Write out one phrase per line.** Indent and start the next phrase on a new line. Keep it up until you finish your sentence. If your sentences routinely con-

tinue for more than five lines—that is, they're longer than five phrases—you're not writing in an oral style. Make your sentences shorter. And vary their length.

- **Never carry a sentence over to a second page.**
- **Double space between major ideas.** (Unlike written pieces that are constructed in paragraphs, speeches are built around ideas and images and stories.)
- **Make notes in the margins or in the text to help your delivery.** Put a double slash mark (//) to remind yourself to pause. Write "breathe" or "smile" or "eye contact" or "slow down" where and when appropriate.

Here's how the opening line of the Gettysburg Address would look:

> *Four score and seven years ago*
> *our fathers brought forth upon this continent*
> *a new nation*
> *conceived in liberty*
> *and dedicated to the proposition*
> *that all men are created equal.*

When you've finished writing it, read it aloud to yourself again and again. I suggest you stand and walk around while doing so. (This simulates the actual speaking situation more closely, and for some reason it makes memorizing easier.) You're not trying to commit the speech to memory, but you do want to take it to heart. Memorize the opening few sentences and the last few sentences. There may be a few other brief passages—images or particularly well-written phrases—that you'll also want to commit to memory.

Now go back and prepare another outline that you can take to the podium with you. Keep it short, no longer than one page. Make the words large. Jot down only a few words for each point, words that will jog your memory. Don't write out sentences.

Then speak from the outline. What you'll find is that once the writin' is done, the talkin' comes much easier.

ANY QUESTIONS ABOUT Q&A?

Many speakers are intimidated by the idea of fielding questions from the audience. They're afraid they won't know the answer.

Undoubtedly, they'd find the Q&A part of their speeches easier and less stressful if they could arrange for the audience to ask only the questions they want to be asked. But—for a leader—that would be wrong to do, as numerous politicians have found out when they were caught planting softball questions.

Actually, letting the audience ask questions is one of the best ways to engage their interest. It respects their experience and insights. It saves your talk from being a one-way conduit of knowledge. And it keeps you on your toes. If you can't handle questions from the audience, your listeners will think—rightly or wrongly, mostly rightly—that you lack either the conviction or the intellectual rigor expected of a leader.

Q&A is also one of the best ways to drive home your message. You should almost always make Q&A a part of your speaking. A speech wouldn't be a speech without an introduction and a conclusion. And for the most part, it wouldn't be a speech without Q&A.

Sometimes, of course, it's inappropriate to take questions from the audience. For instance, if you only have 5 minutes to speak, you'll want to stand up, make your point, and sit down. And some speeches simply don't call for Q&A. Like inspirational speeches. When you're stirring people's hopes and dreams, the last thing you want to do is encourage them to ask questions, a process that is by its nature rational, not emotional. And you wouldn't take questions, of course, during a eulogy or a tribute.

I used to think that I'd done a poor job when the audience had a lot of questions after one of my talks. If I'd covered my topic adequately, I reasoned, no one would have any follow-up. They'd sit there, I hoped, in silence, awed at how insightful and comprehensive my talk was. Now I feel just the opposite: The fewer questions I get, the more critical I am about my speech.

That's because a good speech makes people think. It evokes questions. Or more accurately, a good speech evokes *good* questions. (If audiences ask a lot of ill-informed or off-the-topic questions, it's usually because you've confused them.)

You can entertain questions just about anytime during a presentation or, more formally, near its end. But you need to prepare for them just as you prepare every other part of the speech. List all the questions you'd like to be asked as well as the ones you might be asked. Then prepare an answer for each. For the tougher, more critical questions, write out your answers and commit them to memory.

The most important question to ask yourself when you're brainstorming what queries you might get is this: What's the killer question that I most want *not* to be asked? If it's a question that your audience has a right to ask and you're not prepared to answer, your only choice is not to allow them to ask questions at all. And, of course, that's not a good situation.

Here's a rule, however: Never end a speech with Q&A. You can take questions toward the end, but plan on finishing your speech, giving your conclusion, *after* you've answered the last question. Why? Because if you finish your speech and then take questions, you'll get some good questions and some not-so-good ones. The good ones usually get asked right at the start. As you continue taking questions, you're likely to get lamer ones, and the last question you get asked is usually the lamest of all. If you simply answer it and then say, "Well, thank you for your questions" and sit down, you've finished your speech on a very weak point. And, instead, you want to end on your most powerful, most memorable point.

So it's much better to finish your speech with what I call a *soft close*. Summarize your main points and emphasize why it's important that your audience do something or believe something. Then ask for questions. Answer them. Leave yourself 30 to 45 seconds at the end to deliver your *hard close*. This is the one you've carefully scripted and memorized. It has punch. It appeals to the emotions. And it lets the audience leave feeling empowered.

Thus, Q&A, if you approach it in the right way, can be used to reinforce, clarify, and expand on your central theme as well as to involve the audience. Careful planning makes the difference.

Some other points to consider when planning your Q&A:

- **Set the rules at the beginning.** Let the audience know when and how you'll handle questions. Unless you're giving a formal speech to a large audience or are expecting objections, be prepared to take questions throughout your talk, not just at the end. You might, however, want to save Q&A for specific times during your presentation. Whatever you decide, let the audience know.

• **Field questions fairly.** Listen to the entire question. Understand what's being asked—the factual basis of the question as well as the intention behind it. Figure out what the person really wants to know. If necessary, repeat the question so everyone can hear it. Don't embarrass the questioner, but correct any factual errors or misunderstandings immediately. Give all audience members a chance to ask questions.

• **Answer questions tactfully.** Begin by addressing the person who asked the question. Then turn away and talk to the entire audience, so you don't get caught in a one-on-one dialogue. Be respectful of the questioner; avoid sarcasm, criticism, or arrogance. Keep your sense of humor. Answer the question as directly as possible without being abrupt—but don't be afraid to say, "I don't know." (And then offer to get back to the person with the answer.)

• **Remain in control.** Postpone questions that require long answers. If possible, give a brief answer, admit there's more to be said, and offer to discuss it more fully later. You may be able to turn certain questions back on your audience by asking, "What's your experience with this type of situation?" Admit that certain questions will take you too far off topic, but agree to talk with the person after your presentation (if possible). Stay in control, deciding when to cut off questions and move on.

THE PROBLEMATIC QUESTIONERS

Sooner or later, someone will try (consciously or otherwise) to derail your presentation, prove you wrong, or assert their own importance (and their supposedly superior expertise). It's your job to keep control of the situation, not as a power trip but as a service to the entire group. Here are the archetypes and how to defuse them:

- **Nitpickers** quibble with facts and details, raising objections to minor points of your talk. If possible, answer their questions briefly and refocus on the bigger picture. If you're confident about the facts, stand by them. If you don't know for sure, admit the possibility of disagreement. Do not argue with them. Say something like, "I'm not sure about the precise figure. If you see me afterward and give me your card, I'll get back to you with the answer. But I can say this about the bigger issues raised by your question . . ."
- **Naysayers** will contest everything you say. Because they can't be satisfied, don't try. Your responsibility is to address every *fair* objection to your presentation, not to convince everyone. Avoid being rude or visibly angry. Try this: "You've raised some valid questions that I'm afraid we don't have time to discuss fully. If you see me afterward, I'll address them in more detail. I'd like to spend more time right now on the more fundamental issue you raise . . ."
- **Long-winded lecturers** launch into a lecture of their own, never getting

around to posing a question. The trick for you is to reassert control without being rude. Because they rarely come to a full stop, you may need to interrupt them in mid-sentence. Pick up on what they're saying and bring the subject back to your main point.

- **"I-know-more-than-you" experts** will cite obscure facts, sources, or statistics that you can't possibly know. Avoid getting into a who's-smarter-than-who contest. Admit you don't know what they're talking about. Ask them to summarize it briefly and to explain how it relates to the issue at hand. (It usually doesn't.)

- **Usurpers** want to take over the event. Don't let them. If they're unwilling to let you continue without being interrupted, enlist the audience's aid by saying, "It seems that this person would like to change the direction of this presentation. I'd like your input. Would you like to hear him/her out? Or would you like me to continue?" Listeners will inevitably take your side, tell the person to be quiet, and give you permission, if the usurper continues to interrupt, to say, "I'm sorry but I'm going to have to ask you to be quiet or leave."

Here are two ways to encourage audiences to ask questions. First, instead of asking, "Does anyone have any questions?" (which lets people off the hook), ask, "What questions do you have?" This lets people know you presume they have questions and you want to hear them. And second, if people are reluctant to ask questions, you can get them started by using this technique. If people simply sit there and you know they have questions, say, "Here's a question I often get asked." State a question, as if someone is asking it. Then answer it. And here's the trick: Follow up your answer by asking, "Who else has a question?" People who are reluctant to ask the first question have less hesitation about asking the second one.

So don't shy away from questions. Questions give you a chance to reinforce the central theme of your talk, and they might give you new insights as well. In fact, people who think they know all the answers haven't yet been asked all the questions.

MURPHY WAS RIGHT
(THINGS WILL GO WRONG)

Give enough speeches and you're sure to have your share of Maalox Moments. Maybe the microphone dies, a fire alarm goes off, somebody in the audience gets sick, or you totally forget everything you were going to say.

Count on it. Sooner or later, Murphy's Law will come into play, and something will go wrong. It might be a glitch (a mechanical malfunction), a blunder (a speaker miscue), or a mishap (an emergency). But whichever, it's how you handle the crisis that determines whether your speech dies right there on the spot or regains its momentum.

The good news is, no problem needs to be fatal. In fact, you may even be able to use something that goes wrong as a way to improve your speech.

But first, understand that when you do the other things I've suggested and forge a connection with your listeners, they'll become your partners. They'll want you to succeed. When you feel that audience support—when you sense they're on your side—you can relax, trust yourself, and maybe even enjoy the opportunity to speak to them. You're much less likely to make mistakes in the first place if you're at ease. But if foul-ups do occur, you know you can call upon the audience for help.

If and when things do go awry—whether it's of your own doing or beyond your control—your first defense is good planning. Act like a good Boy Scout or Girl Scout—"Be Prepared."

For instance, if you lose your train of thought or your place in your speech, don't get discouraged. It happens even to seasoned professionals. But you don't have to let it sabotage your presentation. Try these techniques:

- **Check your notes.** Keep your notes—at least an outline—within easy reach. Don't call attention to the fact that you've forgotten where you are. Simply pick up your notes, look at them, and begin speaking again. (If there's a glass of water nearby, take a sip from it. The audience will get the impression that you planned it all.)
- **Back up.** Blanking out happens most commonly at a transition point. You've finished your second point, for example, and can't remember your third point. Simply summarize your previous point. Repeat it, if you have to. Doing so will often give you momentum that'll carry you over your memory gap to your next point.
- **Ask the audience for help.** Say, "I got so caught up in what I was saying that I lost my place. Where was I?" Some people will probably laugh sympathetically. Laugh with them. If you gave them an overview of your main points in your introduction, there'll be someone in your audience—count on it—who will know what your next point is and will yell it out. (Involving your

audience like this is a good thing, not a defect. It strengthens your bond with them.)

If you find yourself frequently forgetting your next point, I suggest looking at how you go about constructing your speech in the first place. You may be trying to accomplish too much in a single speech. Or you may have made it overly complicated. Or you may be doing a poor job of logically connecting your main points, one to another.

Forgetting your place in a speech is worrisome enough. What's really terrifying is having a total mental meltdown. If you've ever completely blanked out, forgetting not only what you were going to say but also how to form a coherent sentence, you're not alone. Here's what you can do to keep it from escalating.

• **Take a breath.** Without being aware of it, you may have stopped breathing. (It happens.) Your brain, temporarily deprived of oxygen, shuts down. Breathe. Then breathe again.

• **Say something, say anything!** The longer you stay silent, thinking your way out of the crisis, the more your anxiety—and the audience's—grows. Stop racking your brain in search of the perfect word. Just say something. Once you're talking again, you can find your way back to where you were when you left off.

• **Move.** Avoid the deer-in-the-headlights trap. Do something physical. Take a step in any direction. Make a gesture. Take a sip of water. Move your body, and your mind will begin moving again, too.

- **Check your attitude.** Perfectionism will shut you down faster than anything else. So forget about giving a flawless presentation. Instead, concentrate on being of service to your audience and fulfilling your purpose to the best of your ability.

It's the nature of gadgets—especially sophisticated gizmos like wireless microphones, projectors, and computers—to go haywire. And they invariably do so at the most discombobulating times and in the most stressful situations.

You can be irritated, exasperated, and inconvenienced by these mechanical glitches, but you really shouldn't be surprised by them. Instead, you should have a plan. For starters, make sure you check out equipment in advance. Then:

- **Have backup available.** Lugging a second microphone, computer, or slide projector to the auditorium will make you seem like a genius when the first one self-destructs. Another idea: Make paper copies of your presentation to distribute as handouts, if needed.
- **Focus on the audience and on your message, not on the problem.** As you work on the solution, keep your audience involved. If you can't quickly resolve the problem, proceed with your presentation as best you can—without whining.
- **Use humor.** Good-natured laughter sets people at ease. Laugh at yourself or the technology, not at the people who are in charge of the event. "A TV can insult your intelligence, but it

takes a computer to make you feel like a total idiot," one speaker quipped. Another, when she realized that her handouts were assembled in the wrong order, joked, "And just when I was going to address the myth of perfection . . ."

• **Go on.** The audience will like you for being a good sport. (If the problem continues to be a major distraction, you may need to alter or drastically cut the length of your speech.)

Emergencies—power outages, fire alarms, earthquakes, or other crises—occur infrequently but can really knock a hole in your game plan. Because your audience will look to you for guidance, you should know what to do.

In large gatherings it's wise to have the meeting planner or emcee—not the main speaker—tell the audience where the emergency exits are as part of the general housekeeping announcements. At the very least, you should know where the exits are and what to do in case the room has to be cleared.

If the crisis is easily dealt with (a false fire alarm, for example), after you reconvene make a joke of it if possible. For instance, "As I was saying before I was so rudely interrupted . . ."

One man was speaking to a large Florida audience when the power went out. He waited for people's eyes to adjust to the darkness. (Exit signs provided some light.) He said in a very calm tone of voice, "You don't need to see me to hear me, so if it's okay with you I'll keep talking." After several minutes, just as he was telling about a character who was seeking "a sign from above," the lights came on. The audience cheered wildly as if he'd arranged the whole thing. Score one for chutzpah!

If something happens to someone in the audience, attend to that person. When a woman fell over in her seat at a conference, the speaker asked if anyone was competent to help. A doctor and a nurse rushed forward. He asked the audience to take an early coffee break while an ambulance came and took the person away. When the group reconvened, the speaker gave an update on the woman's condition, then said, "If you're too upset to go on, I quite understand. But with your permission, I'll continue." Perfect!

While you can't steer clear of every mini-calamity, you can plan for any number of possibilities. In speaking, as in life, you're not always in control. But you can be in command.

HUMOR IS NO JOKE

Did you hear the one about the speaker who always began his talks with a joke? He bombed big-time.

And so, in all likelihood, will you if you follow the oldest, stupidest piece of advice ever given to speakers: "Always start with a joke."

No one, except maybe a professional comedian giving a humorous speech, should start with a joke. The truth is, humor helps most speeches, but not all. And jokes are something else altogether.

Listeners need time to warm up to you. Even Jay Leno and David Letterman are preceded—off camera—by warm-up acts that get the audience into a laughing mood. If professional comedians at the top of their form need help, what chance do the rest of us stand?

The odds of an audience laughing out loud at your joke right at the start are slim. And if they sit there in stony silence or—worse—if they groan, you may never recover.

When you tell a joke, you're trying to make the audience laugh. Try, instead, to get them to smile or maybe to chuckle. For instance, while accepting an honorary degree from Harvard, Bill Gates, a college dropout, began not with a joke but with a series of amusing, self-deprecatory comments:

- I've been waiting more than thirty years to say this: "Dad, I always told you I'd come back and get my degree."
- I want to thank Harvard for this timely honor. I'll be changing my job next year . . . and it will be nice to finally have a college degree on my résumé.
- I'm just happy that *The Crimson* has called me "Harvard's most successful dropout." I guess that makes me valedictorian of my own special class . . . I did the best of everyone who failed.
- I want to be recognized as the guy who got [Microsoft CEO] Steve Ballmer to drop out of business school. I'm a bad influence. That's why I was invited to speak at your graduation. If I had spoken at your orientation, fewer of you might be here today.
- Radcliffe was a great place to live. There were more women up there, and most of the guys were science-math types. That combination offered me the best odds, if you know what I mean. This is where I learned the sad lesson that improving your odds doesn't guarantee success.

His comments weren't uproarious, but they did the job. They got people chuckling, and they made Gates—one of the world's richest men— seem like one of them. (Beginning with five self-deprecating comments is a bit much. Gates got away with it because he's so wildly successful. The rest of us mere mortals would be better off limiting ourselves to one or two such remarks.) You can bet that with his wooden delivery style, Gates surely would have flopped if he had cracked a joke.

Humor in a speech can play many roles. As a social lubricant it builds warmth and rapport between you and your audience, lowering whatever resistance they might feel toward you and your ideas. "Humor is gracious and shows respect," Peggy Noonan has written. "It shows the audience you think enough of them to want to entertain them."

Humor puts your listeners at ease, which is especially important if you are addressing a topic your audience might find challenging or discomforting. At the time Carnegie Mellon computer professor Randy Pausch was asked to give a university-wide lecture, everyone knew he had been diagnosed with terminal pancreatic cancer. He clearly did not want them to feel morose or pitying, so he began his speech by saying, "This lecture series used to be called the last lecture. If you had one last lecture before you died, what would it be?" He paused. Then he smacked his hands together and said, "Damn, I finally nailed the venue." The audience laughed. His gentle humor allowed them to let go of whatever apprehension or awkwardness they may have been feeling.

Humor also makes your points more memorable, and it may allow you to steal ammunition from your critics. "A year ago my approval rating was in the thirties, my nominee for the Supreme Court had just withdrawn, and my vice president had shot someone," George W. Bush told the lighthearted Radio and Television Correspondents' Association Dinner in 2007 as his poll numbers continued to plummet. "Ah," the president added, "those were the good ol' days."

The easiest way to put appropriate humor into your speech is to poke fun at yourself—as Gates and Bush did—or to share personal experiences.

Laugh at yourself, your foibles, your mistakes, and you make it easier for the audience to laugh quietly with you. So mention something amusing that happened to you or your family or your organization—just be sure it illustrates a point in your speech.

HOW TO USE HUMOR

To be amusing without appearing to try too hard, follow these rules:

- **Be yourself.** You can learn from your favorite comics, but don't imitate them. Instead, hone your personal brand of humor. And trust your instincts: If you don't think a line or a story is funny, don't use it.
- **Rehearse.** It takes practice to use humor so well that it sounds spontaneous and unscripted. So test out your material first in front of safe audiences.
- **Keep it clean.** Avoid anything listeners might find embarrassing, insulting, or offensive. You want people laughing with you, not at someone. Once you offend an audience, it's hard—if not impossible—to win them back.
- **Write it out.** A sense of surprise, clever wordplay, exaggeration and embellishment, amusing anecdotes, ironic twists—in fact, all aspects of humor—get better with the kind of refinement and precision that comes from writing and rewriting. If you're lucky enough to say something unexpectedly funny or off script, write it down afterward so you can use it again.
- **Don't tell listeners what's funny.** Saying, "This is really funny" is a setup for failure. Simply tell your story or make your witty remark and allow the audience to respond. If they laugh, great. If they don't, move on.

- **Don't use humor for its own sake.** Use it to reinforce or illustrate your main points. Or use it to change the emotional tone of your speech or to signal a change in direction.

Should you ever tell a joke *in* a speech, not at the beginning?

Yes, you can *if* you're a good and practiced joke teller—you regularly tell jokes in everyday situations and people regularly laugh. Or, *if* the audience is expecting you to tell jokes. And *if* the joke is appropriate for the audience, the occasion, and the message, and *if* you're prepared to respond if your listeners don't laugh.

But that's a whole lot of "ifs." So my advice on making jokes at the beginning or anywhere else in your talk is: When in doubt, don't.

As for humor, it pays to err conservatively there, too. Always remember that humor can offend as well as delight. So ask yourself the "AT&T" questions: Is it Appropriate? Is it Tasteful? Is it Timely?

Even if your humor meets those criteria, remember: Less is more. So keep it short. Avoid long stories or complicated setups. And limit how often you use humor. After all, as amusing as you can be, you still want to be taken seriously.

PROJECTING POWER

Today's audiences don't want leaders to be domineering or coercive. They aren't simply willing to listen and follow orders. Instead, they want to be wooed and won over. Yet they don't respect leaders who appear tentative or weak or seem to crave an audience's approval. Listeners only respect leaders who speak with a strength that's confident, but not arrogant, and bold, but not brash.

Of course, many ways exist to project this type of strength. Which way you use has a lot to do with what kind of person you are in your unguarded moments, with how you exercise leadership on a day-to-day basis, and with your reputation. But you can do things physically while you're speaking that will enhance the audience's perception of your strength. These include the way you stand, move and gesture, and dress.

- **The way you stand.** You don't want to look as though you can be pushed over or pushed around. You want to look solid and grounded, like a person capable of standing strong against the winds of change and opposition.

   So work from the ground up. Begin by planting your feet hip-width apart. Distribute your weight evenly on your feet, front to back and side to side. Don't lock your knees. (When you're nervous, locking your knees will make your legs shake more noticeably.) Tuck in your pelvis to eliminate an excessive arch in the lower back. (Imagine that you're zipping up a pair of pants that are too tight.) Lift your sternum. Roll your shoulders back. Tuck your chin down slightly. Raise your head as high as possible, as if someone were pulling the hair on the top of your head near the back. Leave your hands by your sides.

Opera singers stand like this in order to project their voices so powerfully. Stage actors stand in the same way. Even if you don't think of yourself as an entertainer, you can learn from them. Stand strong and your audience will see you as strong.

This default stance—the position you return to when you're not moving or gesturing—may feel unnatural at first. That's not because it *is* unnatural but because it's uncustomary. Until you become accustomed to standing this way, know that you look both natural and strong. Soon enough, you'll get used to it.

• **The way you move and gesture.** There are as many ways to move and gesture while speaking as there are speakers. But here are two basic guidelines: First, be yourself. And second, be purposeful.

Be yourself. The more you focus on communicating your message, on connecting with your audience, and on accomplishing your goal, the more you'll be yourself. And the more natural you are, the less you'll need to invest thought and energy into how to move and gesture.

Many speech coaches will disagree, but I think choreographing your movements and gestures in anything more than a general way is counterproductive. It'll make you look staged, stiff, and unnatural. I've heard horror stories about speech coaches and teachers who, like drill sergeants, upbraided speakers for the way they moved. One speaker was told that she "talked Italian"—that is, that she used her hands too much. She was forced to practice speaking with her arms tied to her sides. And another had his pockets stapled shut so he couldn't put his hands in them. Like others who are ridiculed for their actions, they didn't change—at least not in a good way. They simply became more intimidated by speaking.

If you want to move and gesture more powerfully, be natural. And the best way to be natural is to be confident.

Be purposeful. Whatever you do, have a reason for doing it. Pacing from side to side, rocking back and forth, using the same gesture repeatedly out of sync with anything you're saying—all of these are meaningless movements. Don't do them.

Instead, coordinate your gestures with your words. And move in sync with your speech. You might, for example, finish off one point while facing one side of the audience. Then, just as you're about to transition into your next point, move slightly on the stage and look at another part of the audience. Or when you're telling a story that involves a dialogue between two people, move your body slightly to face different directions each time you speak as a different person.

The easiest way to observe how you move while you're speaking is to videotape yourself in action. Then watch the video in fast-forward. (I said it was *easy*, not pleasant.) Doing so will call attention to your habitual way of moving and will highlight any movement or gesture that looks unnatural.

• **The way you dress.** The rule of thumb is to dress a little more formally than your audience. That's a good rule to follow most of the time. But I find it more helpful to suggest that you dress the way the audience expects you to dress. (Typically but not always, they'll expect you to dress a little more formally than they do.) The president of a construction firm, for example, doesn't have to outdress the investment bankers he's addressing.

It's sometimes hard these days to know how to dress. In the past you couldn't go wrong in business circles, at least, if you dressed in formal business attire. For men, that typically meant a dark suit, a light shirt, and a nonflashy tie. For women, a business suit (either a skirted suit or a tailored pantsuit) with leather shoes (closed-toe/closed heel) would suffice. But now all bets are off. When you're speaking to an audience you don't know, ask the meeting planner to describe what the audience will be wearing. Make the planner be specific. Don't accept general terms like "casual attire" or "business attire." "Casual" covers a multitude of variations, depending on the part of the country, the economic status of the audience, and their profession. When in doubt, dress more formally than you think you need to. You can always remove a coat or make some on-the-spot adjustment to appear less formal.

Casual dress is more difficult to pull off than you might think. And it's often more expensive. I worked with a client who frequently spoke at events with California governor Arnold Schwarzenegger and other state leaders at groundbreaking ceremonies. Most people, including the governor, tended to dress down for these events. After all, they were expected to don hard hats and pose with shovels in their hands.

After observing several such events, however, I had to tell my client that he was greatly underdressed. "But I'm in chinos and an open shirt like everyone else," he said. "Yes," I agreed, "but you look shabby standing next to a man whose every article of clothing is tailor-made." The personal shopper at a high-end department store was able to help him find clothes that were more suitable for similar occasions.

If you speak frequently, I suggest that you have two or three outfits that you use almost exclusively for the times you speak: something formal, something casual, and something in between. Don't scrimp. Get help in selecting these outfits. Keep them clean and well pressed and ready to go.

GESTURES TO AVOID

Some gestures should be avoided when you want to project strength. They inherently make you look weak. They're never natural or confident.

- **The fig leaf.** When you cross your hands low in front of you, as if you're a statue covering your private parts, you can't help but look weak or, worse, scared.

- **Wringing hands.** Clutching your hands and wringing them, usually at navel height, communicates nervousness and indecision. It never looks strong.
- **Praying hands.** Clasping your hands in a folded position as if you are praying only makes you look like you're begging for mercy. Don't do it.
- **Wagging finger.** You'll look like a scold, not a leader. (Also, avoid the Bill Clinton variation. He used to wag his finger at audiences all the time until someone convinced him to stop. He couldn't eliminate the gesture entirely, so he ended up bending his forefinger and wagging his knuckle.)
- **The magic wand.** If you hold anything in your hand, especially if it is thin and long, you'll tend to wave it about as if it were a wand. That's one more reason not to use a pointer of any sort. And keep pens out of your hand.
- **The flapping chicken.** This is what you look like when you pinch your elbows to your side, hold your forearms and hands straight out, and move them from front to side as if you were taking flight.
- **The endless loop.** Even the strongest gesture loses power if it's overused.

Power, according to the ancient Greek philosophers, is not the strength to overwhelm or subdue others, but the ability to create or accomplish something worthy of praise. That's certainly true when it comes to leaders wooing their audiences. Use every resource at your command to project this kind of power, and your listeners will respect you for it.

WHEN YOU MUST
USE POWERPOINT

A friend of mine sneaks an occasional cigarette. "Don't say a word," she admonished me recently, knowing what I think of her smoking. "Yes, it's a filthy habit, and yes, it's going to kill me if I keep it up, but sometimes you just gotta."

That's my attitude toward using PowerPoint. There are so many reasons to avoid using it—especially if you want to have the kind of impact leaders have on their audiences—but sometimes you just gotta.

First, a quick recap of some of the reasons for not using it.

In the first place, it is best suited for presenting information, not for influencing or inspiring an audience. There's a debate among academicians and the like about PowerPoint's usefulness. The minority opinion holds that PowerPoint is inherently flawed. It doesn't allow enough information to be clearly presented. You'll find this out for yourself the first time you cut and paste a chart or graph from a written report straight into a PowerPoint slide: it becomes unreadable. This causes presenters to resort to my all-time least-favorite line, "You probably can't read this, but . . ."

And PowerPoint doesn't require you to make connections or to tie the bits and pieces together. You can project a slide, talk about it, and then say my second-least-favorite line, "Next slide." You don't have to—most presenters don't—tell the audience how all the information you're presenting on different slides fits together. There may be a clear and obvious connection in your mind—after all you're the expert and you know how it all fits together—but PowerPoint doesn't make the connection. It keeps the pieces in pieces.

PowerPoint proponents, on the other hand, praise its effectiveness in presenting information and say that if the information is poorly served by bullet points, indecipherable graphics, and a disjointed message, the problem is with the speaker, not the software. Long before PowerPoint, proponents rightly point out, audiences suffered through boring and confusing talks. It's just a tool and its effectiveness—or lack thereof—is determined by how it's used.

Whether you agree with the critics or with the advocates, notice what both sides are arguing about: the effectiveness of PowerPoint in communicating *information*. Neither side believes PowerPoint will help you shape how an audience thinks and feels or stir them to action. And that's mainly what leaders want to do.

There's another reason leaders shouldn't use PowerPoint: It hogs people's attention. When you project something on the screen, people look at it. Even if it's nothing more than a list of bullet points. Even if they can read it in 20 seconds flat and you keep it up for 2 minutes. They'll keep looking at it. And all the time they're looking at it, they're not looking at you. People who lack confidence or who aren't concerned about being thought of as a leader actually like that about PowerPoint. They like it when the audience isn't looking at them. But as a leader, you don't want to be upstaged. You want people to look at you.

And there's a practical reason for shunning PowerPoint. It's time-consuming. Sure, you can produce great looking slides. Al Gore did it with the presentation he used in *An Inconvenient Truth*. (Actually, he used Apple's version of slideware, called Keynote.) His presentation cut between professionally produced photographs, video clips, animation, and graphics. And it looked great. Mind you, he had a production team of Hollywood talent helping him and a budget few people have at their disposal. Left to your own devices, you'll probably spend more time formatting slides than thinking through your strategy or crafting your message. And even then you'll end up with slides that today's visually sophisticated audiences will find boring.

Okay, you probably already know that using PowerPoint isn't the best choice for someone who wants to convey a sense of authority while speaking. But like my friend with her occasional smoke, sometimes you just gotta.

Sometimes, you have to present information. Yes, yes, yes, you should be more concerned about influencing and inspiring your audience. But there are times when, even as a leader or maybe especially as a leader, it's your responsibility to communicate information. At times, executives have to explain financials to their boards. Senior researchers have to give technical updates. Program managers have to make oral proposals for large contracts. And small business owners and self-employed entrepreneurs have to make sales presentations.

And sometimes, audiences simply—and adamantly—require you to use PowerPoint. There are audiences, especially in the high-tech arena, who simply cannot conceive of a presentation that doesn't involve Power-Point. It's almost as if they won't take you seriously if you don't show up with a laptop and projector. You could, arguably, do a better job getting your message across to them without using PowerPoint, but you'd have to fight their assumptions to such a degree that it isn't worth it.

MAKING THE BEST USE OF POWERPOINT

Well-designed visual aids—used well, appropriately, and in small doses—can make your presentation clearer and more memorable if you follow these rules:

- **Make them visible.** The main point of using visual aids is, duh, to let people see them. But it's surprising how often at least some members of the audience can't see them. The graphics are too small, too distant, or hidden behind a post or the heads of other audience members.
- **Make them visual.** Graphs, charts, diagrams, photographs, illustrations, maps, video clips, and the like appeal to the eye. They're easy for the mind to understand. Words—especially long sentences or bullet-point lists—are something else entirely. People have a hard time reading while listening; don't make them choose between you and your slides.
- **Use fewer of them.** There's no need to put your entire presentation on the screen, and there's no need to use a slide for every point you want to make. Eliminate slides that don't advance your message, like the cover slide and the agenda slide. Use your slides only to clarify, explain, or substantiate your main points.

- **Blank out the screen whenever possible.** Begin your presentation simply speaking to your audience, with nothing on the screen. (In PowerPoint, the screen will go black when you press the B key, white when you press the W key. Hit any other key and the screen will turn back on.) Bring up a slide when appropriate, talk to it, and then blank out the screen and continue talking.

- **Talk to the audience, not the slide.** Look at your listeners at least 80 percent of the time. Never turn your back to the audience.

- **Avoid clip art.** It's almost always amateurish.

- **Avoid pointers.** If you need to use a pointer, it's usually because your visual is too complex or confusing. Simplify it. If you still have to point, use your hand. (Besides, once you get a pointer in your hand you'll be tempted to wave it around like a wand when you're not pointing to something or, if it's a laser pointer, to highlight every word on the screen.)

- **Explain the aid's content when you first show it.** As soon as you show an object, your listeners will look at it even if you're still talking about something else. Don't confuse them by having a slide up that has nothing to do with what you're saying.

When you have to use PowerPoint, use it sparingly and to your advantage. Keep it in its place, so it doesn't upstage you. And remember, even when you're presenting information, you—your body, clothes, grooming, actions, gestures, facial expressions, and demeanor—are the most important visual aid. And you—not the slides—are the media and the message. Everything else is and should be secondary.

LIFE AFTER POWERPOINT

A CFO came to me for help with her presentations to the board of directors. The CEO was planning to retire, and she wanted to be considered for the position. But she was concerned about the feedback she'd received from the board. Its members said they respected her and her performance, but they weren't sure she was "CEO material." When she asked one member what that meant, he said, "The only time we really see you is during your presentations. Which are impressive. You're organized, clear, and you address all our issues. I can honestly say I've never understood our financial reports as well as I do now. But a CEO needs to give people a vision and fire them up. And we just don't know if you can do that."

She was caught in a bind. On the one hand, the board expected her to speak about the company's financials, go into a lot of specifics, and explain their implications. All of which can be pretty dry. And at the same time they wanted her to paint the bigger picture and generate more excitement. We worked out a strategy for her to try at the next meeting.

She brought her chief financial analyst to that meeting. She began the talk, without PowerPoint, speaking directly to the board about the firm's financial situation, its challenges, and its possibilities for future growth. Then she called the analyst forward and remained standing a little to the side while he used ten PowerPoint slides to review the company's finances in detail. Together she and the analyst answered the questions raised by the board. Then she thanked the analyst who sat down, and she concluded with a brief statement about her vision of the company's future direction.

The jury's still out on whether she'll get the CEO job. But she felt much happier about her performance, and I suspect she's improved her chances.

What the CFO's new strategy allowed her to do is what communications experts and political advisers call *framing*. A frame is an overarching system of assumptions, values, and standards—a worldview—that gives meaning and purpose to particular elements and events. Her financial analyst gave the details. He explained, as objectively as possible, in a way that could be justified to an auditor, "Just the facts, ma'am." She provided the frame. She gave a way—*her way*—of understanding the facts and of how to act as a result.

The moral of the story is if you want to be perceived as a leader, you have to provide not just the facts, but the frame as well.

WEANING YOURSELF OFF POWERPOINT

You may not be able or even want to avoid using PowerPoint entirely, but you'll reinforce people's perception of your authority if you lessen your dependence on it. Here are some ways to reduce, if not eliminate, your reliance on Power-Point.

- **Avoid giving presentations that would require you to use PowerPoint.** Begin with the conviction—people expect leaders to have convictions—that using PowerPoint is somehow beneath you. Palm off any presentation that involves PowerPoint onto someone else.

- **When you do use PowerPoint, cut down on the number of slides you use.** The typical advice is to plan on one slide per minute or two of talking. Try instead to use as few slides as possible, no more than eight or ten per presentation. (And remember to blank out the screen when you're not referring to what's on it.)

- **Use other ways to communicate information.** Depending on the size of the audience, their expectations, the time available, and the meeting space, there may be much better ways to present information than PowerPoint. Consider using a whiteboard, an electronic whiteboard, or a flip chart. They allow you to draw diagrams or make lists as you're speaking. (And if someone gets up from the audience and adds to what you've drawn, all the better.) Or distribute handouts. None of these alternatives is as attention-grabbing as PowerPoint, and that's the point. They allow you to present information without having to compete for your audience's attention.

In spite of the common adage, the facts don't speak for themselves. They need to be gathered, assessed, analyzed, understood, and explained. That's what leaders do. It's okay—and often necessary—for a leader to present information in a speech. But what will set you apart from the others is how you frame that information.

When FDR addressed Congress and the nation following the attack on

Pearl Harbor, he presented a lot of information. He listed, for example, the other places attacked by the Japanese: Hong Kong, Guam, the Philippines, Wake Island, and Midway Island. Yet he wasn't presenting the information for its own sake. He really didn't care if anyone even remembered it the next day. What he did care about was the meaning of the information, its implications, and ultimately its call to action. In 1941, while the rest of the world was at war, most Americans resisted being drawn into a conflict they thought had nothing to do with them. Roosevelt had a different perspective, and he used it to frame his message to the American people. We have been attacked unjustly and without provocation, he asserted, by an empire bent on conquest. We must defend ourselves. We must go to war.

You may not be the president of the United States addressing an entire nation. You may not be the president of a company, an executive, or even a manager. But if you have any desire to speak in a way that grabs people's attention, affects how they think and feel, and stirs them to action, you can learn from the way great leaders speak. Provide the frame for understanding, not just the facts.

Now Break the Rules

When Demosthenes, the greatest of Greek orators, was asked what the three tests of a great speech were, he answered, "Action. Action. Action." For a leader today, the answer would be "Results. Results. Results."

As a leader you speak to forge the identity of your audience, to influence how they feel and think about important issues, and to inspire them to take action. All the rules of speaking exist to help you accomplish one or more of those goals.

But understand, rules are not, of themselves, important. *Results* are.

Speaking is more an art than a science. And as with any art, there are rules and principles and guidelines for speaking, most of which have evolved through twenty-five centuries of real-life practice, study, and revision. They include:

- Know what you want to accomplish.
- Be prepared.
- Build rapport with your audience.
- Appeal to your listeners' emotions and intellect, to their imaginations and values.

- Speak briefly and to the point.
- Know that who you are speaks as loudly as what you say.

Address an audience without applying these basic rules, and you're setting yourself up for failure. Yet rules and principles and guidelines only get you so far. They're neither absolute laws that must be obeyed in each and every situation nor rigid principles that, if followed, will guarantee success.

Masterful speakers, like their artistic counterparts, break the rules—even the big ones—from time to time. But they don't break *all* the rules. What's more, they *know* what rules they are breaking and why.

If you disregard all the rules, you'll end up with an amorphous mess that bears little resemblance to a speech. In such a case, you'd be better off not giving a speech at all. Do something else instead. Circulate a memo, a position paper, or an e-mail. Call a meeting, hold a conversation, sponsor a workshop, produce a video, run an ad campaign, host a website, or write a blog. All are legitimate means for communicating and—depending on the situation and on what you want to accomplish—any one of them could be a better choice than giving a speech.

Break the rules of speaking out of ignorance—the important ones, at least—and you'll expose yourself as an amateur or a dilettante. And you'll sabotage any chance of success.

There's only one rule that, while not an absolute, you should almost never violate: Know what you want to accomplish. All the other rules are simply ways of helping you achieve your goal. They're means to an end. And, of course, it's the end that matters.

In November 2001, former president Bill Clinton spoke to the students at Georgetown University. He let his mind—and the minds of his audience—range over a host of ideas. He spoke about history, democracy, the new world economy, the purpose of education, the changing face of warfare, and the need to engage Islam in a dialogue.

Long and wordy, the speech addressed too many issues, never quite weaving them together into a meaningful whole. It was more than a little self-justifying. And yet it was a good speech because it achieved its purpose, it produced the sought-after result. It gave hope to an anxious student body—and, by extension, to an anxious country—less than two months after the terrorist attacks on the World Trade Center and the Pentagon.

In the final analysis, results are the only yardstick. For instance, the founder and president of an investment brokerage firm asked me to help him develop more confidence while he was speaking. He often met with the CEOs and presidents of small-to-midsize companies and with money-management executives. He was young, and he felt intimidated around professionals he thought were more experienced and knowledgeable.

I listened to what he was already doing and made a number of suggestions. I also told him that the kind of confidence he was seeking often came only with lots of experience. But he kept coming back to his nervousness.

"The next time you speak," I suggested, "don't focus on your nervousness or on how to overcome it. That's like telling yourself not to think about an elephant. Focus, instead, on achieving the outcome you want."

When we met again, he reported on what he considered at least a middling success. "I don't know if I was any more confident. I wasn't paying attention to that. But I do know I got the results I wanted and that's good enough for now." *Exactly.*

To keep today's audiences engaged, the rule is that you should speak briefly (under 20 minutes) and focus tightly on one and only one idea. But rule or no rule, occasions come up when you may want, like Clinton, to spend more time, leisurely sharing your thoughts—and your thinking process—about any number of loosely connected issues. Not every speech has to sound like an executive briefing.

To stay connected to your audience and to keep your delivery from sounding flat, you should avoid reading your speech. That's another rule. But one of the most moving inspirational speakers I've heard—Patricia Livingston—fine-tunes a script for every speech and then reads it word for word.

Another rule: Telling a story will improve just about any speech. But not *every* speech. Similarly, taking a stand is the sign of a leader. But not all the time. And real leaders should never use PowerPoint. Except sometimes when they should.

If you're consistently getting the results you want from your speeches, then, as far as I'm concerned, you're a good speaker. You may not have the resonant voice you'd like or a commanding presence or an easy way of interacting with your audience. But none of that matters if you're achieving your goals.

If, on the other hand, you're unhappy with the response you're getting from audiences, you many need to return to the basics.

You can speak extemporaneously or read from a script word for word. You can saw wildly at the air with your arms or clench the lectern with white-knuckled hands. You can lose your place, forget an important point, trip over your words, sweat profusely, and fumble your answer to an easy question. You can talk longer than expected, running over the allotted time. You can address too many ideas and lose the audience for whole stretches of your speech. You can be afraid of looking your audience in the eye. Yes, you can even use PowerPoint.

All is forgiven. All is well *if,* when you're finished speaking, your listeners know and feel and do what you want them to.

[EXEMPLARY SPEECHES]

"And Ain't I a Woman?"

In 1851 Sojourner Truth, a former slave, an abolitionist, and a women's right activist, addressed the Ohio Women's Rights Convention in Akron, Ohio. I choose her speech—"And Ain't I a Woman?"—because it has three characteristics I admire in a leader's speech. First, Truth's *voice*—its crispness, immediacy, and bite—is utterly distinctive. No one else could say what she said without sounding like a fraud or like an actor playing a role. Second, her speech gives you a sense of who she is: a woman who has lived through a lot and never once considered herself a victim. And finally, how could you not be mesmerized by the power of the refrain, "And ain't I a woman?" Notice, also, the concreteness of her images.

Well, children, where there is so much racket there must be something out of kilter. I think that 'twixt the negroes of the South and the women at the North, all talking about rights, the white men will be in a fix pretty soon. But what's all this here talking about?

That man over there says that women need to be helped into carriages, and lifted over ditches, and to have the best place everywhere. Nobody ever helps me into carriages, or over mud-puddles, or gives me any best place! And ain't I a woman? Look at me! Look at my arm! I have ploughed and planted, and gathered into barns, and no man could head me! And ain't I a woman? I could work as much and eat as much as a man—when I could get it—and bear the lash as well! And ain't I a woman? I have borne thirteen children, and seen most all sold off to slavery, and when I cried out with my mother's grief, none but Jesus heard me! And ain't I a woman?

Then they talk about this thing in the head; what's this they call it? [member of audience whispers, "intellect"] That's it, honey. What's that got to do with women's rights or negroes' rights? If my cup won't hold but a pint, and yours holds a quart, wouldn't you be mean not to let me have my little half measure full?

Then that little man in black there, he says women can't have as much rights as men, 'cause Christ wasn't a woman! Where did your Christ come from? Where did your Christ come from? From God and a woman! Man had nothing to do with Him.

If the first woman God ever made was strong enough to turn the world upside down all alone, these women together ought to be able to turn it back, and get it right side up again! And now they is asking to do it, the men better let them.

Obliged to you for hearing me, and now old Sojourner ain't got nothing more to say.

"THE RACE IS OVER, BUT THE WORK NEVER IS DONE"

In 1931 the leaders of politics, the arts, and science took their places before widely scattered microphones to pay tribute to Oliver Wendell Holmes, the highly respected Supreme Court Justice, on his ninetieth birthday. At the end of the program, Holmes gave a brief, extemporaneous speech in response. Although addressed to an unseen radio audience of several million people, it has the feel of something intimate—an old man passing on a bit of wisdom that he has gleaned over the years. It sounds as if it comes from his heart to one other person's ears: yours. It is both humbling—a highly accomplished, ninety-year-old-man exhorting us to keep working—and encouraging as he inspires us to live, really live.

In this symposium my part is only to sit in silence. To express one's feelings as the end draws nigh is too intimate a task.

But I may mention one thought that comes to me as a listener. The riders in a race do not stop short when they reach the goal. There is a little finishing canter before coming to a standstill. There is time to hear the kind voices of friends and to say to oneself: The work is done. But just as one says that, the answer comes: "The race is over, but the work never is done while the power to work remains." The canter that brings you to a standstill need not be only coming to rest. It cannot be, while you still live. For to live is to function. That is all there is to living.

And so I end with a line from a Latin poet who uttered the message more than fifteen hundred years ago, "Death plucks my ear and says: Live—I am coming."

"Taxi to the Dark Side"

In 2007 Alex Gibney won the Academy Award for best documentary feature for *Taxi to the Dark Side,* an examination of the torture practiced by the United States in Afghanistan, Iraq, and Guantánamo Bay. The film focuses on an innocent Afghan taxi driver who was tortured and killed in 2002. I offer Gibney's acceptance speech as proof that it's possible to make a powerful, brief statement on an occasion when everyone expects speeches to be long, boring, and inane. It exemplifies one of the most telling characteristics of a leader's speech: Gibney takes a stand, a gutsy one, unafraid of other people's responses. He lets his passion—his outrage and his love—show.

Wow. Thank you very much, Academy. Here's to all doc filmmakers. Truth is, I think my dear wife Anne was hoping I'd make a romantic comedy, but honestly, after Guantánamo, Abu Ghraib, extraordinary rendition, that simply wasn't possible. This is dedicated to two people who are no longer with us: Dilawar, the young Afghan taxi driver, and my father, a navy interrogator who urged me to make this film because of his fury about what was being done to the rule of law. Let's hope we can turn this country around, move away from the dark side and back to the light.

INDEX

CHRISTOPHER WITT has used over a quarter century of professional speaking experience to help CEOs win board approval and company-wide support for their initiatives and turn technical experts into speakers anyone can understand. He is the founder and president of San Diego–based Witt Communications and holds a doctorate from Catholic University of America.